D-DAY

A Photographic History of the
Normandy Invasion

Martin K. A. Morgan

Front cover:
V Corps troops land from an LCVP on the Easy Red sector of Omaha Beach near the Ruquet Valley at about midday on June 6. On the beach are a DUKW amphibious truck and three M3 Half-tracks, two of which are towing M1 57mm antitank guns. Men can be seen moving up the bluff in the background as the 115th Infantry Regiment pushes south toward Saint-Laurent-sur-Mer, which was still held by the remnants of 716 Infanterie Division and 352 Infanterie Division. *National Archives and Records Administration/US Army Signal Corps 111-SC-190641*

Back cover:
Top: A group of soldiers from the 359th Infantry Regiment, 90th Infantry Division bound for Utah Beach on LCI(L)-326 on D-Day afternoon. The man in the front is carrying his M1 Garand rifle packed in a Pliofilm bag to protect it from sand during the landing, and he carries an 81mm mortar round in its cardboard transport tube threaded through the chest straps of his M1928 Haversack. A U.S. Coast Guard–manned landing craft, the 326 was built by Brown Shipbuilding Corporation in Houston, Texas, in 1942. *U.S. Coast Guard Collection in the U.S. National Archives 26-G-2402*

Middle: The Allen M. Sumner–class destroyer USS Meredith (DD-726) had been in service for less than three months when she sailed as part of the Western Naval Task Force in June 1944. On the morning of June 6, Meredith was assigned to the fire support area off of Utah Beach, at which point she fired her first shots in anger.

Bottom: With a DUKW in the background, a member of the U.S. Navy's 2nd Beach Battalion tinkers with a captured German Goliath tracked mine, or "beetle," on Utah Beach on June 11, 1944. The Goliath was a radio-controlled mini tank that let the user remain under cover while sending explosives into enemy lines to detonate them. *U.S. Navy photograph, now in the collections of the US National Archives 80-G-252752*

On the frontis:
A soldier from the 1st Battalion, 8th Infantry Regiment carrying an M1917A1 Heavy Machine Gun and a belt of .30-caliber ammunition passes through La Madeleine after landing on Utah Beach. The house behind him served as the command post for Oberleutnant Matz, the German officer from 3, Grenadier Regiment 919, who commanded Widerstandsnest 5. This machine gunner still wears his lifebelt and assault gas mask bag. Attached to his M1936 Pistol Belt is an M1911A1 .45-caliber Pistol in its holster and an M1910 entrenching tool. *National Archives and Records Administration/US Army Signal Corps 111-SC-190466*

Brimming with creative inspiration, how-to projects, and useful information to enrich your everyday life, Quarto Knows is a favorite destination for those pursuing their interests and passions. Visit our site and dig deeper with our books into your area of interest: Quarto Creates, Quarto Cooks, Quarto Homes, Quarto Lives, Quarto Drives, Quarto Explores, Quarto Gifts, or Quarto Kids.

© 2014 Zenith Press
Text © 2014 Martin K. A. Morgan

This edition published in 2019 by Crestline, an imprint of The Quarto Group, 142 West 36th Street, 4th Floor, New York, NY 10018, USA
T (212) 779-4972 **F** (212) 779-6058 **www.QuartoKnows.com**

First published in 2014 by Zenith Press, a member of The Quarto Group, 401 Second Avenue North, Suite 310, Minneapolis, MN 55401 USA

Crestline titles are also available at discount for retail, wholesale, promotional, and bulk purchase. For details, contact the Special Sales Manager by email at specialsales@quarto.com or by mail at The Quarto Group, Attn: Special Sales Manager, 401 Second Avenue North, Suite 310, Minneapolis, MN 55401, USA.

10 9 8 7 6 5 4 3 2 1

ISBN: 978-0-7858-3692-6

Editor: Elizabeth Demers
Design Manager: James Kegley
Layout Designer: Becky Pagel
Cover Designer: Rachael Cronin

Printed in China

MIX
Paper from responsible sources
FSC® C104723

CONTENTS

To the memory of

Joe Wilson Morgan, III

March 5, 1963–February 21, 2010

Introduction

THE PHOTOGRAPHIC RECORD is priceless. As the Normandy invasion grows more distant in the mirror of history, the pictures remain with us, almost an uncompromising keepsake to that extraordinary, remarkable event. The pictures illustrate what we read in the original documents or the veterans' memoirs, or the words we hear as we listen to their personal stories. The photos provide us with definition and context. They humanize what is now a legendary event. Each photograph conveys only a single moment in time, a second of experience, a glimpse into the reality of that instant. They cannot and do not tell us all, but they do tell us something honest. The photographs show us the uniforms, the weapons, the equipment, the hairstyles, the food, the setting, even the time of day on that momentous June 6, 1944. More interesting, the best of them convey the mood and the emotions of the participants. They show the fear, the anticipation, the confusion, and, in some instances, the camaraderie of a particular moment.

The photographs of the Normandy invasion—many of them familiar to most anyone who has studied D-Day—have created unforgettable images in our minds and, for many of us, they have inspired myriad questions. Where was this photo taken? Who are the soldiers in the image? What was their mission at the time? What happened to them? Did they notice the photographer taking their picture? How did they feel about that? Martin K. A. Morgan has spent years gathering and studying the images. He has walked the hallowed invasion beaches countless times. He has dug deeply into archives in multiple countries, poring over image after image. Over the years, he has befriended large numbers of veterans, many of whom have been kind enough to trust him with their own pictures. Suffice it to say his expertise on the photographic record of the Normandy invasion is formidable and impressive. Thus, Martin's captions provide quite a few answers to our age-old questions. As you leaf through this handsome book, you will undoubtedly see numerous familiar photographs and you might be tempted to think you know the story behind them and their proper context. With all due respect, you would most likely be wrong in that assumption. Martin has taken those familiar images and made them new again because of his truly remarkable level of knowledge and insight. He has also succeeded in presenting many new or previously little-known photographs among the pages that follow. So, sit back and enjoy a fresh look at one of history's most significant events, as seen through the keen eyes of the talented photographers of yesteryear and a fine historian of our own time.

John C. McManus
St. Louis, MO
Author of *The Americans at D-Day* and
The Dead and Those about to Die: D-Day, June 6, 1944, the Big Red One at Omaha Beach

Author's Introduction

THE D-DAY INVASION OF NORMANDY in 1944 remains one of the most famous combat operations of World War II. In seven decades, countless histories have examined various aspects of this pivotal battle, from broad focus to close detail. While the sheer number of titles available seems to suggest that everything the world needs to know about D-Day has already been written, the reality is quite the opposite. Mythology and hyperbole swirl around the subject, producing historical distortions that continue to interfere with a balanced and nuanced understanding of June 6. For example, despite what countless bad television programs will tell you, D-Day was not the largest invasion in history. For that matter, it was not even the largest amphibious landing operation of World War II. That record belongs to the Operation Iceberg landings on Okinawa in 1945. Although not the biggest, the airborne component of June 6, 1944, definitely made it the most complicated invasion of World War II. But in a modern cultural environment where every subject seems to have a hyperbolized narrative, the Normandy invasion is no exception.

In the United States, the general atmosphere of hyperbole and mythology attending much of the popular historical writing and programming about D-Day has tended to emphasize the American contribution. To be perfectly clear, the U.S. military did not fight D-Day alone. It fought as part of a multinational coalition force consisting of twelve allied nations that came together to complete a challenging and intimidating mission. Although this is certainly not a revelation, the most popular books and motion pictures of the last two decades have memorialized the American side of the D-Day narrative to such a great extent that the other Allies are in need of some advocacy. It might even come as a surprise to some to learn that Lt. Gen. Miles Dempsey's British 2nd Army put more people ashore on June 6 than Lt. Gen. Omar Bradley's U.S. 1st Army did (83,000 versus 73,000). By 1944, the German military had become multinational as well. In addition to its ethnically German troops, the *Wehrmacht* fighting force in Normandy included foreign volunteers, conscripts, and laborers from Italy, Poland, Czechoslovakia, the Soviet Union, Georgia, Spain, and even France itself. In the end, National Socialist Germany failed to create a war-winning coalition among its *Ostlegionen* (Eastern legions) and *hilfswilligen* (voluntary assistants), but these non-Germans were nevertheless an important part of the D-Day story that many may not be fully aware of.

An infatuation with the events of Tuesday, June 6 alone has also exerted itself on the D-Day historical narrative. While the events of that day offer up irresistible drama to the world of popular history, events before and beyond June 6 are as compelling. It is for that reason this book concentrates on some of the most notable events that occurred during the week of the invasion. The way the battle unfolded in the American sector during that week was documented in hundreds of photographs. The majority of these images were taken by official U.S. Army, Navy, and Coast Guard photographers; men who went to war with cameras in their hands. But there were also privately owned cameras in abundance during the Normandy invasion, and they recorded a more intimate and personal side of the fighting. This book presents 450 of the most compelling and dramatic photographs captured in England before and during embarkation and in northern France during its liberation. Many of the images in the pages that follow are familiar, but for too long they have been treated anonymously and not placed within the proper context of time or place. Others have not been published previously and therefore offer something new to even the most well-read D-Day enthusiast. I have sought to make a contribution to the scholarship of this subject by identifying precise locations where photographs were taken and, whenever possible, the people who appear in them. In many cases, even the name of the man behind the camera is listed. It is my hope that this information will be useful to others who love D-Day history as much as I do. The rich details revealed in the captions for these photographs represent years of work done in close collaboration with several experts on the subject, namely Sean Claxton, Adam Berry, Paul Woodadge, and Niels Henkemans. I am also deeply indebted to Brian Siddall and Mark Bando, both of whom command levels of knowledge and expertise that continue to inspire me to work harder. Adam Makos and Barrett Tillman were both generous with their time and advice, and I am indebted to them both for that. Finally, I am grateful to Dr. John C. McManus for writing an arresting introduction that provides this book an added level of credibility.

Chris Naylor and Lee Steed from the Homewood High School class of 1988 expressed a mutual enthusiasm for this subject that encouraged me at a crucial moment. Jeff Tucker and Colin Colbourn likewise had nothing but uplifting words as I worked toward completion. Were it not for Dr. Gayle Wurst, Dr. Elizabeth Demers, and Erik Gilg, *The Americans on D-Day* would still just be another one of my bright ideas. This book would not have been possible without the support of C. Paul Hilliard of Lafayette, Louisiana, and special thanks are therefore reserved for him. Nancy L. Scott was mission critical as both a proofreader and a life partner—thank you, Nancy, for being with me throughout this project. Finally, thank you to Joe and "Pete" Morgan for being the most supportive parents in the world.

Martin K. A. Morgan
Slidell, Louisiana
September 2013

The BUILDUP

"An Overrehearsed Play"

The U.S. military started preparing for D-Day many years before it actually took place. A full national mobilization began even before Pearl Harbor, when President Franklin D. Roosevelt signed the Selective Training and Service Act of 1940. After Germany declared war on the United States on December 11, 1941, the process of preparing for D-Day got under way full scale. Across the country, new military camps and training grounds appeared rapidly as the government attempted to expand the size of U.S. fighting forces with the greatest speed possible.

LEFT: Soldiers from the U.S. Army's 2nd Infantry Division mug for the camera during a training operation in the United Kingdom shortly before D-Day. Although they all wear standard infantry uniforms and equipment, some of these men also carry two pieces of specialized gear issued to troops involved in amphibious landing operations: the U.S. Navy inflatable invasion lifebelt and the M7 Assault Gas Mask Bag (worn over the chest). The soldier in the center front has his GI mess kit tucked under his left armpit, and the man to his right is using an M1936 canvas Musette Bag as a pillow.

The buildup of U.S. military forces in the United Kingdom began two years before the Normandy invasion. Here, a local police sergeant provides directions to 1st Sgt. Elco Bolton near Radford, England, on June 17, 1942. A native of Muscogee County, Georgia, Bolton enlisted in the army on January 17, 1939, in response to a recruiting drive for the Territory of Hawaii. Three years later, he was a senior NCO in a quartermaster trucking company near Birmingham in the West Midlands. First Sergeant Bolton is armed with the formidable M1928A1 Thompson Submachine Gun.

U.S. Army soldiers receive familiarization training on the use of the M7 Grenade Launcher in England shortly before the invasion. Introduced in February 1943, the M7 made it possible to launch various types of grenades with the M1 Garand rifle using the M3 .30-caliber Rifle Grenade Cartridge (a blank cartridge specifically made to propel rifle grenades from rifle-grenade launchers). In this photograph, the soldier kneeling in the center is about to fire off a Mk II fragmentation hand grenade mounted on his M1 rifle with an M1 Grenade Projection Adaptor. The soldier standing to his left has just pulled the pin on the hand grenade, the final step before firing.

The U.S. Army's airborne units exemplify the swift expansion of U.S. fighting forces after hostilities began. Most of the paratroopers who jumped into Normandy on D-Day had received their basic training in the immediate aftermath of Pearl Harbor. Thus, the critical time period associated with America's entry into the war and the masses of volunteers in late 1941 and early 1942 is also a period importantly associated with June 6, 1944. But, in addition to the preparations connected to training troops to expand the size of the military, American industry was building toward D-Day as well. Chrysler, Ford, Boeing, and other giants of industry produced the large-scale weapons—the tanks, trucks, and bombers—that Allied forces would eventually use in combat in northern France. U.S. businesses also produced small weapons at a breakneck pace. Although the Springfield Armory and Winchester were producing the semiautomatic M1 Garand service rifle as quickly as they could, there still were not enough to go around. The result was the distribution of a large number of M1903 bolt-action rifles to the troops who would ultimately come ashore on D-Day. Before the rifles, tanks, and troops could reach the beach, however, they had to reach Europe, and to do so, they needed ships. Kaiser Shipyards on the West Coast, Brown Shipbuilding in Texas, Alabama Drydock and Shipping in Mobile, and Bath Iron Works in Maine all built the fleet that would provide invaluable service during the invasion. In the New Orleans area, Higgins Industries produced one of the mission-critical tools for the eventual cross-channel invasion: landing craft. Although small in stature,

ABOVE: Two U.S. Army soldiers from A Company, 121st Engineer Combat Battalion, 29th Infantry Division participate in a training exercise in England before the invasion. They are assembling sections of the infamous Bangalore torpedo, a demolitions weapon that was particularly effective at blowing gaps in barbed-wire entanglements. *National Archives and Records Administration/US Army Signal Corps 111-SC-184811* **LEFT:** U.S. Army soldiers use a Jeep to move a Very Low Altitude (VLA) antiaircraft balloon during a training exercise in southern England before D-Day. The VLA balloon could be moored to the ground or to a ship by a heavy mooring cable, but its lift was not particularly strong, so it could be moved using the method depicted here. The VLA balloon provided a simple yet effective means of preventing enemy aircraft from conducting strafing or dive-bombing attacks. *National Archives and Records Administration/US Army Signal Corps 111-SC-179839*

ABOVE LEFT: A field full of U.S. Army M1 40mm Automatic Antiaircraft Guns and M1A1 90mm Antiaircraft Guns awaits the cross-channel attack that will bring them into contact with the enemy. Sights like this were common across England during the buildup toward D-Day. Each weapon is covered with a canvas tarp to prevent exposure to the elements. *National Archives and Records Administration/US Army Signal Corps 111-SC-189322* **ABOVE RIGHT:** A lone soldier looks out over a field full of M3 37mm Antitank Guns and M1A1 90mm Antiaircraft Guns during the buildup of military equipment in England prior to the Normandy landings. *National Archives and Records Administration/US Army Signal Corps 111-SC-189324*

ABOVE LEFT: Ford GPA amphibious utility vehicles and Dodge WC-51 Weapons Carriers sit in a field in England waiting for the impending invasion that will take them to France. By this stage of the war, the U.S. Army was a thoroughly mechanized fighting force that would soon become a critical part of a sweeping war of maneuver in northwestern Europe. *National Archives and Records Administration/US Army Signal Corps 111-SC-189323* **ABOVE RIGHT:** A U.S. Army corporal takes inventory of a warehouse storing rope bundles. Although not usually considered an important part of the U.S. Army's military might, rope would become a valuable commodity during the campaign that followed the D-Day landings. *National Archives and Records Administration/US Army Signal Corps 111-SC-189805*

ABOVE LEFT: U.S. Army soldiers stack bundles of Square Mesh Track (SMT) that will be used as a surfacing material in the construction of advanced landing grounds in France after the invasion. *National Archives and Records Administration/US Army Signal Corps 111-SC-189363*

ABOVE RIGHT: African-American U.S. Army soldiers stack bundled sections of Perforated Steel Planking (PSP) at a supply depot in England shortly before D-Day. Sometimes referred to as "Marsden" or "Marston" matting, PSP was a standardized, perforated-steel matting material developed to facilitate the rapid construction of temporary runways and landing strips. Sections of this matting could be easily interlocked to provide a stable, all-weather surface that could facilitate the swift establishment of advanced airfields. PSP was a critically important asset supporting the projection of airpower over northern France. *National Archives and Records Administration/US Army Signal Corps 111-SC-189325*

ABOVE LEFT: This view of the engineer depot at Thatcham, Berkshire, shows some of the different types of construction vehicles being amassed in England prior to the invasion. Here, Allis-Chalmers HD10W tractors, Caterpillar D4 tractors, and Caterpillar D7 bulldozers can be seen parked together in anticipation of the journey toward Germany. *National Archives and Records Administration/US Army Signal Corps 111-SC-189366* **ABOVE RIGHT:** Two soldiers inspect the inflation cylinders on U.S. Army rubber rafts in England before D-Day. *National Archives and Records Administration/US Army Signal Corps 111-SC-189806*

these vessels were of the greatest import because they would make it possible to transfer personnel and equipment from big ships in deep water across the open beaches.

For all the contributions of the factories and training areas back in the United States, preparations for D-Day played out in the United Kingdom in earnest. There the war created a clash of cultures as service personnel from several nations descended on the islands during the pre-invasion buildup. From Northern Ireland to Wales, Scotland, and England, the United Kingdom became a maneuver area for the air, ground, and naval forces that would one day be called on to liberate Europe. The preparations for D-Day were so thorough and frequently repeated that newspaper correspondent Alan Moorehead described them as "an overrehearsed play," indicating an anxious impatience to get the show on the road. For the British, who had experienced the war in a completely different way than the Americans, the reality was stark: since 1940, they had experienced bombings, food rationing, and fear of invasion. They had endured the loss of family and friends in addition to the absence of thousands of British soldiers, sailors, airmen, and Marines who were overseas serving in Asia, North Africa, or the Mediterranean. For them, total war was not a distant abstraction they read about in headlines—it reached across the English Channel from the continent. Then, the Americans began arriving in 1942. U.S. troops by the tens of thousands had come to prepare for the assault on fortress Europe. In the United Kingdom, cities swarmed with young American men who had not yet experienced war in the way the British had. But that was about to change.

Perhaps the best remembered aspect of the Operation Fortitude deception effort that preceded D-Day was the inflatable Sherman tank. By populating phony marshaling areas with these decoys, the Allies could trick German photoreconnaissance interpreters into believing they were assembling armored forces in areas of England where they were not actually doing so. The overall objective of this subterfuge was to "induce the enemy to make faulty strategic dispositions of forces." (This quote comes from the Plan BODYGUARD Deception Policy operational order dated December 25, 1943. It is available through numerous sources, including a complete reprint in *Fortitude: The D-Day Deception Campaign* by Roger Hesket.)

Meanwhile, in France

During the months that preceded June 6, the French experienced the full landscape of hardships associated with being an occupied country. On an almost daily basis, Allied aircraft subjected northern France to heavy

OPPOSITE: Landing craft were among the most important weapons needed to carry out the Normandy invasion, and American industry answered this requirement by mass-producing a variety of different models. This photograph, taken at the beginning of 1944, shows the Bayou St. John testing area for New Orleans–based Higgins Industries. Here, Higgins boats were tested before being delivered to the military. Among the models seen here are the Landing Craft, Support (LCS) (small); the Landing Craft, Personnel (LCP) (large); the Landing Craft, Vehicle, Personnel (LCVP); and the seventy-eight-foot Higgins PT Boat. On the left, three LCVPs have been loaded onto railroad flat cars for over-land transportation.

"*This is your worry here—this is it.*" A U.S. Army soldier cleans his M1903 bolt-action rifle in a camp in England shortly before the Normandy invasion. Although the U.S. Army had adopted the semiautomatic M1 Garand rifle in 1937, a large number of M1903s were still being issued in 1944.

bombardment. In an effort known as the "Transportation Plan," these bombings targeted the enemy's means of movement. Bridges, railroad marshaling yards, rolling stock, and highways were rapidly reduced to rubble in an attempt to degrade Germany's ability to move equipment and personnel in response to an invasion. While targets like the battery at Pointe du Hoc and the Fortress of Mimoyecques near Landrethun-le-Nord in the Pas-de-Calais region were easily hit from high altitude, others were well concealed and, therefore, less obvious. This resulted in collateral damage among French civilians, who, by this time, had endured the often harsh realities of life under German occupation for years. Throughout this time period, rationing, curfews, deportations, and even reprisals were part of everyday life. There were even employment offices that existed only to recruit young French people to relocate to Germany to do jobs that had been left vacant by the Third Reich's war effort. But, in the background of all of this activity, the French Resistance was becoming an increasingly active and dangerous network of saboteurs and spies that challenged the German occupation.

U.S. Army soldiers billeted on the grounds of the English castle seen here in the background drive through the estate's gate on the way to an invasion training session on April 18, 1944. In addition to having become a sprawling supply depot, by 1944, England had also become one vast maneuver and training area. Note that a censor has scratched out unit information beneath the right headlight of the M8 Greyhound armored car that is just passing through the gate.

U.S. Army troops pass British civilians as they march toward their embarkation port shortly before D-Day. In this interesting photograph, the men can be seen wearing M1937 Olive-Drab Wool Field Trousers, M1937 Olive-Drab Flannel Shirts, Russet Service Shoes, and Leggings. One man is carrying an M1 2.36-inch rocket launcher (or "bazooka") while the rest all seem to be carrying the M1 Garand rifle. One of the soldiers is in mid-salute, while the driver of the sedan on the left is displaying the "V" for victory sign. Behind that is a Ford GP (or "Jeep") being driven by an African-American soldier. Farther back in the road column a GMC CCKW 2.5-ton Cargo Truck follows a Harley-Davidson WLA Motorcycle.

Waiting and the Weather

D-Day was not scheduled to be Tuesday, June 6, 1944. It was scheduled to begin on Monday, June 5, but during the weekend a front moved in over the English Channel, bringing heavy rain, strong winds, and high seas. The operation was postponed by twenty-four hours because of the weather. General Dwight D. Eisenhower made the decision to postpone during a meeting at his headquarters at Southwick House, which was the advance command post of the Supreme Headquarters of the Allied Expeditionary Force (SCHAEF) near Portsmouth in Hampshire County. At the time of the postponement on Sunday, June 4, Eisenhower instructed the staff to reconvene the following day to determine if meteorological conditions had improved. When the team assembled again on Monday, June 5, Group Captain J. M. Stagg (SCHAEF chief meteorologist) reported a probable break in the weather. Eisenhower then polled the staff to consider their opinions about whether or not to go, and there was a 50/50 split. Despite this, Eisenhower believed it was time for "ramming our feet into the stirrups," so he gave the order to begin the operation by saying, simply, "OK, let's go."

A column of trucks from B and C Batteries, 32nd Field Artillery Battalion pauses on the side of a road in southern England as it moves toward the port of embarkation in June 1944. The GMC CCKW 2.5-ton Cargo Truck in the center of the photograph is towing an M2A1 105mm Howitzer marked *Djebel Berda* and *Mt. Etna*, indicating that it saw combat in Sicily the previous summer. The 32nd Field Artillery provided artillery fire support for the 1st Infantry Division during the battle for France.

General Dwight David "Ike" Eisenhower, Supreme Commander of the Allied Expeditionary Force. Ike ultimately gave the order to begin Operation Neptune/Overlord by saying "OK, let's go" at Southwick House near Portsmouth in Hampshire.

General Eisenhower, Supreme Commander of the Allied Expeditionary Force. His instructions for the upcoming cross-channel invasion, and the drive toward Germany itself, were outlined in a simple, thirty-word operational order: "You will enter the continent of Europe and, in conjunction with the other united nations, undertake operations aimed at the heart of Germany and the destruction of her armed forces."

ABOVE: General Bernard Law Montgomery answers questions from war correspondents at his command post on the grounds of Château de Creully near the town of Creully during his first press conference after the Normandy landings. Although he would soon be promoted to the rank of Field Marshall, at the time this photograph was taken, he held the rank of General in command of the Allied 21st Army Group. *National Archives and Records Administration/US Army Signal Corps 111-SC-190425* **RIGHT:** General Sir Montgomery, commander of the Allied 21st Army Group, and General Eisenhower, Supreme Commander of the Allied Expeditionary Force, pose at General Montgomery's field command post in Normandy on July 26, 1944. These two men exercised overall control of the ground battle in Normandy. In the background is one of General Montgomery's many mascots: a wire fox terrier he named "Hitler." *National Archives and Records Administration/US Army Signal Corps 111-SC-192193*

ABOVE: Landing Craft, Infantry (LCI)-238, LCI-214, and LCI-311 moored together along the waterfront in Weymouth, Dorset, shortly before the Normandy invasion. The buildings in the background at the center of the photograph line Custom House Quay between the Esplanade and Maiden Street. **RIGHT:** An M4A3 Sherman medium tank of the 66th Tank Battalion, 2nd Armored Division backs aboard a U.S. Navy Landing Ship, Tank (LST) in England during the embarkation phase that necessarily preceded crossing the English Channel. Note the U.S. Navy officer perched on the upper hinge of the ship's portside bow door. *National Archives and Records Administration* **OPPOSITE:** A GMC CCKW 353 2.5-ton truck nicknamed "Lil' Nellie" is loaded aboard LST-134 at Portland Harbour in Dorset during embarkation before D-Day. A deep-water fording kit has been installed on "Lil' Nellie," and she has a camouflage net lashed to her left front wheelwell. LST-134 carried elements of the divisional headquarters for the 1st Infantry Division to the Easy Red sector of Omaha Beach on June 6, 1944. **OPPOSITE INSET:** A Jeep is lowered onto a Higgins Landing Craft, Mechanized (LCM)-3 from the *Harris*-class attack transport USS *Joseph T. Dickman* (APA-13).

ABOVE: Loading LST-357 at Portland Harbour in Dorset during embarkation before D-Day. In the foreground, a Dodge WC-51 Winchless Weapons Carrier and a GMC DUKW 353 2.5-ton amphibian truck prepare to come aboard. The emblem above the throat leading to the ship's tank deck depicts a stork (nicknamed "Palermo Pete") and the motto "We Deliver." By June 1944, LST-357 had already participated in the Operation Husky landings in Sicily (July 1943) and the Operation Avalanche landings at Salerno, Italy (September 1943). On D-Day, "Palermo Pete" landed elements of the U.S. Army V Corps on the Easy Red sector of Omaha Beach. **OPPOSITE ABOVE:** A Jeep from the Engineer Special Brigade's medical unit drives aboard a Landing Craft, Tank (LCT) nicknamed "Channel Fever" at Castletown near Portland (south of Weymouth) in Dorset during embarkation for D-Day. **OPPOSITE BELOW:** Jeeps and personnel from the 1st Infantry Division on board the LCT "Channel Fever" at Castletown near Portland (south of Weymouth) in Dorset. Among the soldiers and sailors seen here are two U.S. Navy ensigns (standing shoreside between two soldiers) as well as troops from the 5th Engineer Special Brigade and the 741st Tank Battalion.

ABOVE: Jeeps and personnel from the 1st Infantry Division on board the LCT "Channel Fever" at Castletown near Portland (south of Weymouth) in Dorset. Among the men seen here are a sailor and soldiers from the 5th Engineer Special Brigade and the 741st Tank Battalion. **OPPOSITE ABOVE:** Three U.S. Army combat engineers from either the Special Engineer Task Force or Beach Obstacle Demolition Party move to their embarkation assembly area in preparation for D-Day. Each soldier carries a section of Bangalore torpedo on his shoulder, reels of Primacord, and an M7 Assault Gas Mask Bag worn on his chest. The man in the center already has his M1 Garand rifle packed in a Pliofilm bag to protect it from sand during the landing. *National Archives and Records Administration* **OPPOSITE BELOW:** In this photograph, taken on Thursday, June 1, 1944, U.S. Army Rangers march along the waterfront in Weymouth, Dorset, to meet the landing craft that will carry them to the transports anchored in the harbor. The Rangers remained aboard their ships during the coming days as a security precaution. Here, men can be seen carrying Bangalore torpedo sections, M7 Assault Gas Mask Bags, U.S. Navy invasion inflatable lifebelts, and assault/invasion vests in dark-green canvas (which were distributed ten days before the invasion).

ABOVE: This photograph shows the intersection where Custom House Quay and the Esplanade meet on the waterfront in Weymouth, Dorset. At the time this photo was taken during the first week of June 1944, the embarkation for Operation Neptune was well under way. In the background, LCI(L)-497; LCH-87 can be seen nested together alongside the quay. At the center are two trailers carrying bottles of compressed hydrogen used to inflate VLA antiaircraft barrage balloons like the three secured to the ground with nets and sandbags in the foreground. At center right can be seen an International Harvester 4x4 Truck, a closed-cab GMC 353, a U.S. Navy 6x6, three Dodge WCs, and a Diamond T Model 972 Dump Truck. **OPPOSITE:** Soldiers from the medical section of either the 5th or the 6th Engineer Special Brigade board an LCT at Castletown near Portland (south of Weymouth) in Dorset during embarkation before D-Day.

ABOVE: At the intersection of Custom House Quay and the Esplanade on the waterfront in Weymouth, Dorset, U.S. Army Rangers have begun boarding five Royal Navy Landing Craft, Assault (LCAs) for the trip out to their transport anchored in the harbor during embarkation shortly before D-Day. In the background, LCI(L)-497, LCI(L)-84, and LCH-87 can be seen nested together alongside the quay. **BELOW:** Thursday, June 1, 1944: Two Higgins LCM-3s from the USS *Samuel Chase* (APA-26) have pulled up to the seawall at the intersection of Custom House Quay and the Esplanade on the waterfront in Weymouth, Dorset. In the background, U.S. Army Rangers are loading five Royal Navy LCAs, and LCI(L)-497, LCI(L)-84, and LCH-87 are nested together.

ABOVE: Thursday, June 1, 1944: At the intersection of Custom House Quay and the Esplanade on the waterfront in Weymouth, Dorset, U.S. Army Rangers have boarded five Royal Navy LCAs for the trip out to their transport anchored in the harbor during embarkation shortly before D-Day. In the background, LCI(L)-497, LCI(L)-84, and LCH-87 can be seen nested together alongside the quay. **BELOW:** "Check Rosters Here": U.S. Army Rangers make one last stop in this tent before boarding landing craft that will take them out to the transports that will ultimately carry them to Normandy. After checking in with officers of the Transportation Corps at the front of the tent, the men receive donuts and coffee from the Red Cross at the other end of the tent. The famous Weymouth Pavilion, requisitioned by the military during the war, is visible in the background.

Personnel of the 5th Engineer Special Brigade embarking on a Higgins LCVP from the USS *Thurston* (AP-77) using the portside ramp of LCI(L)-497 on the waterfront in Weymouth, Dorset while a VLA antiaircraft barrage balloon floats overhead.

LEFT: U.S. Army soldiers loading a Higgins LCVP from the *McCawley*-class attack transport USS *Barnett* (APA-5) in Plymouth Harbor during a training exercise prior to D-Day. The LCVP next to it (marked PA13-25) belongs to the USS *Joseph T. Dickman* (APA-13), a *Harris*-class attack transport operated by the U.S. Coast Guard. Both the *Barnett* and the *Dickman* ultimately carried elements of the 4th Infantry Division to Utah Beach on D-Day. At the far left, a group of soldiers has already boarded an unidentified British LCA (probably from *Empire Gauntlet*).

BELOW: U.S. Army Rangers from A Company, 5th Ranger Battalion boarding a British LCA in Weymouth Harbor, Dorset, during embarkation for D-Day on June 1, 1944.

ABOVE LEFT: U.S. Army Rangers from E Company, 5th Ranger Battalion aboard an LCA in Weymouth Harbor, Dorset, during embarkation for D-Day on June 1, 1944. **ABOVE RIGHT:** U.S. Army Rangers from E Company, 5th Ranger Battalion aboard an LCA in Weymouth Harbor, Dorset, during embarkation for D-Day on June 1, 1944. These men have been identified as T-5 Joseph J. Markowitz (with an M1A1 Rocket Launcher), Robert Presutti (partially obscured), and Corporal John B. Loschiavo (on the right with the M1 Garand rifle). At the far left, another Ranger can be seen holding a pack of Lucky Strike cigarettes, and his M1 rifle can be seen directly behind strapped to a section of Bangalore torpedo. **BELOW:** Higgins LCVPs loading troops at Portland Harbour during embarkation before D-Day. The landing craft in the foreground (PA30-13) is from the *President Jackson*–class attack transport USS *Thomas Jefferson* (APA-30). A Diamond T 969A 4-ton 6x6 wrecker can be seen in the background.

ABOVE: Two of LST-351's six Higgins LCVPs pull alongside the ship in the middle of the River Tamar at Plymouth, Devon, during embarkation before D-Day. In the background is the distinctive and easily recognizable Royal Albert railway bridge linking Plymouth to Saltash in Cornwall.

LEFT: A Higgins LCVP from the *President Jackson*–class attack transport USS *Thomas Jefferson* (APA-30) backs into Portland Harbour with a load of U.S. Army soldiers during embarkation before D-Day.

RIGHT: Three Higgins LCVPs pull alongside the *Harris*-class attack transport USS *Joseph T. Dickman* (APA-13) during the embarkation phase of Operation Neptune. *National Archives and Records Administration/US Army Signal Corps 111-SC-190440* **BELOW:** LCA-1377 carries Rangers from the U.S. Army's 5th Ranger Battalion across Weymouth Harbor on Thursday, June 1, 1944, during embarkation for D-Day. This landing craft is boat number one from the HMS *Prince Baudouin*, a former Belgian cross-channel ferry impressed into Royal Navy service as Landing Ship, Infantry (LSI) (small)-488 after escaping from the German invasion in 1940. In the stern of the LCA, a Ranger medic can be seen with Geneva Convention markings on his M1 helmet and a similarly marked 60mm mortar shell case modified to carry medical supplies. The three Rangers in the bow area of the LCA are (from left to right): Lt. Stan Askin from the 1st Platoon of Company B, 5th Ranger Battalion; Capt. John C. Raaen, Jr., of Headquarters Company, 5th Ranger Battalion; and Maj. Richard

P. Sullivan, Executive Officer of the 5th Ranger Battalion. **OPPOSITE:** Men of the legendary 1st Infantry Division prepare to depart southern England for their voyage to France. This image provides details about the uniforms and equipment worn and carried by the soldiers who fought at Omaha Beach on D-Day. The men seen here are mostly wearing M1937 Olive Drab Wool Field Trousers, M1937 Olive Drab Flannel Shirts, and M1941 Field Jackets. Seven of the men seen here are wearing the winter combat jacket sometimes referred to as the "tanker jacket" because it was developed for issue to armored-vehicle crews. While almost everyone is wearing the M1 steel helmet, seven of the men are also wearing the issue M1 Helmet Eyeshields. Several M1 Rifles and M1 Carbines can be seen in the photo, and a few of them have already been encased in their clear Pliofilm protective bags, a necessity for an amphibious landing. The African-American soldier is wearing the M1942 Herringbone Twill (HBT) uniform and is not a member of the 1st Infantry Division but probably the 320th Barrage Balloon Battalion (VLA). The soldier in the foreground with his pants legs rolled up is sitting on a green canvas assault vest.

From the AIR

IN THE MONTHS THAT PRECEDED D-DAY, many elements of the invasion plan were already in motion. Photoreconnaissance aircraft were collecting images of the invasion beaches, and U.S. Army Air Forces (USAAF) and Royal Air Force (RAF) bombers were striking targets on a daily basis in an effort to weaken Germany's ability to produce war materiel. In February 1944, this campaign escalated dramatically during "Big Week" as a series of massive bombing raids sought not only to cripple German industry but also to draw the Luftwaffe into a decisive battle. With air superiority as its main objective, Operation Argument (the official name for the "Big Week" missions) sent bombers and fighters of all shapes and sizes, including the new "bubble-top" P-51D Mustang, skyward to pound factories and airfields across the Third Reich. Then, the so-called "Transportation Plan" was launched against railroads, marshaling yards, rolling stock, and bridges in France with the goal of crippling the German military's ability to move in response to the invasion.

This photograph of the beach at Vierville-Sur-Mer was taken by a USAAF P-38E photoreconnaissance *Lightning* just eighteen days before D-Day.

RIGHT: A 101st Airborne Division paratrooper identified as Corp. Louis E. Laird boards a C-47 Skytrain transport before one of the practice jumps that preceded the Normandy invasion. He is armed with the M1A1 2.36-inch antitank rocket launcher, more popularly known as the "bazooka." In practice during combat jumps, the bazooka was dropped in an equipment bundle and not on the individual to avoid fouling the parachute canopy and risers on opening. Corporal Laird also has a pack of Camel cigarettes tied to his left forearm, but they would certainly not remain there through a static-line jump. He has an M7 Assault Gas Mask Bag, which is visible just below and to the left of his T-5 parachute and an M3 fighting knife in an M8 scabbard strapped to his left calf. **BELOW:** This photograph of the beach at Vierville-sur-Mer was taken by a U.S. Army Air Forces (USAAF) P-38E photoreconnaissance Lightning on May 19, 1944, just eighteen days before D-Day. Two of the simplest yet most effective types of German beach obstacles can be seen here: the timber flip-over obstacle and the infamous Czech "hedgehog" antitank obstacle.

While all of this was happening, U.S. airborne forces used the time to continue their preparations for D-Day. Physical and individual training followed an unrelenting schedule through the winter of 1944, but then in the spring, airborne troops participated in several mass tactical exercises designed to acquaint the men with the full scale of the upcoming operation. Exercise Eagle, which was held May 9–12, 1944, is a perfect example of the large-scale training that preceded D-Day. It was the 101st Airborne Division's dress rehearsal for the Operation Neptune assault against German-occupied France, and it took place in Wiltshire between the villages of Hungerford and Newbury. For this exercise, the 101st used the same airfields they would later use for D-Day, and a large number of the unit's men sustained injuries. At the end of May, all of the soldiers who would participate in the airborne component of Neptune were moved to their embarkation airfields and sealed in before their final briefings. On May 29, USAAF ground crews across England received orders to paint "invasion stripes" on all aircraft (with the exception of heavy bombers). It was hoped that the three white and two black stripes would prevent friendly fire incidents during the upcoming operation. Painting them on the wings and tails of almost everything that would fly on D-Day became an added sign that something of great consequence was about to happen.

The characteristic bend of the D517 coast road at Vierville-sur-Mer was photographed by a USAAF P-38E Lightning almost a full year before D-Day. In less than twelve months' time, this area would be designated the Dog Green sector of Omaha Beach, and it would be the scene of intense fighting at the very outset of Operation Overlord. Because of the weapons of the Widerstandsnest 72 defensive complex, the U.S. Army's V Corps would suffer very heavy casualties here on June 6.

Monday, June 5, 1944

The June 30, 1943, photoreconnaissance sortie showed the eastern side of the draw at Les Moulins between Vierville-sur-Mer and Colleville-sur-Mer. This area would become beach exit D-3 in the Easy Green sector of Omaha Beach the following year by the U.S. Army and would be the scene of significant combat action between German defenders in Widerstandsnest 66 and men of Maj. Sidney V. Bingham, Jr.'s 2nd Battalion, 116th Infantry Regiment, 29th Infantry Division. Villa Les Sables d'Or is the three-story house on the left near the water's edge.

Since the amphibious element of the invasion had already departed harbors in southern England and Wales, the only element still in England on June 5 was the airborne. In addition to bombers, fighters, and reconnaissance aircraft, the invasion force included two U.S. Army airborne divisions: the 82nd Airborne and the 101st Airborne. With a combined strength of over seventeen thousand men, they were to assault into various drop zones and landing zones between the Vire River and the Merderet River on the Cotentin Peninsula using parachutes and gliders. The week before the invasion, the various units were moved to and sequestered at embarkation airfields in England in anticipation of the coming D-Day invasion. During the day on Sunday, June 4, they began preparing for their night drop (which was to be the next day), but then they received the stand-down order when General Eisenhower elected to postpone the operation. They began preparing all over again on Monday, June 5, and then began taking off just after sunset, which was at 10:06 p.m. that time of year. A few minutes after midnight on Tuesday, June 6, the U.S. airborne operation began when pathfinders from the 101st Airborne Division started landing north of Carentan.

ABOVE: A Republic P-47D-15-RE Thunderbolt (s/n 42-76141) from the 350th Fighter Squadron, 353rd Fighter Group, Eighth Air Force that has already been painted with the D-Day invasion stripes. Captain Lonnie M. Davis nicknamed the aircraft "Arkansas Traveler" when he was assigned to it shortly after D-Day. **BELOW:** Lieutenant Colonel Joseph B. McManus of the 383rd Fighter Squadron, 364th Fighter Group, 67th Fighter Wing poses on the wing of North American P-51K Mustang (s/n 44-11762) "Clam Winkle" at an Eighth Air Force base in England. This photograph was taken on March 10, 1945, so invasion stripes have not yet been applied to the aircraft.

ABOVE: Some of the 56th Fighter Group's most accomplished pilots: front row, Lt. Col. Francis S. "Gabby" Gabreski (61st Fighter Squadron), Capt. Robert S. Johnson (61st Fighter Squadron), Capt. Walker M. Mahurin (63rd Fighter Squadron), Col. Robert B. Landry (56th Fighter Group commanding officer); back row, Capt. Walter Cook (62nd Fighter Squadron), and Lt. Col. David C. Schilling (62nd Fighter Squadron/Group Headquarters). These men would fly long fighter sweeps over the invasion beaches on June 6, 1944. **RIGHT:** Three men from a USAAF fighter group's maintenance section servicing a North American P-51 Mustang at a base in England in early 1944. The man closest to the camera is loading belted M2 .50-caliber cartridges into one of the ammunition trays for one of the aircraft's ANM2 .50-caliber machine guns. With an intense air war unfolding in the skies over northwestern Europe, the maintainers of aircraft were just as important as the pilots who did the flying.

LEFT: Lieuttenant General Lewis H. Brereton, commanding general of the U.S. Ninth Air Force, poses with the "Luckiest Bomber in the Ninth Air Force" at USAAF Station 485, Royal Air Force (RAF) Andrews Field. Martin B-26B-25 "Mild and Bitter" (s/n 41-31819) of the 452nd Bombardment Squadron, 322nd Bombardment Group (Medium) became the first Marauder flying from England to complete one hundred combat missions over the Continent after it returned from an afternoon raid on the German airfield at Evreux/Fauville, southwest of Rouen, France, on May 8, 1944. Ninth Air Force Bomber Command aircraft (like this one) were central to the crescendo of tactical bombing activity that preceded D-Day. *National Archives and Records Administration/US Army Signal Corps 111-SC-194520*

ABOVE RIGHT: The members of the aircrew of B-17G (s/n 42-31103) "Pegasus, Too" review a chart before a mission in early 1944. Assigned to the 563rd Bombardment Squadron, 388th Bombardment Group (Heavy) based at Knettishall in Suffolk (USAAF Station 136), this Flying Fortress went on its first mission in July 1943. "Pegasus, Too" was ultimately lost on its thirty-third mission following a collision with an enemy aircraft over Steyerberg in Lower Saxony on March 23, 1944, during the bombing raids that preceded the D-Day invasion. **ABOVE LEFT:** Bomber air crewmen synchronize their watches during a briefing on June 20, 1943. They are from the 91st Bombardment Group (Heavy), an Eighth Air Force B-17 unit operating from USAAF Station 121 at Bassingbourne in Cambridgeshire. Although the 91st operated as a strategic bombardment group during most of its time in England, it would eventually fly tactical bombing missions in support of ground forces in Normandy during the months of June and July 1944.

LEFT: A formation of U.S. Ninth Air Force B-26 Marauder medium bombers retiring to the north after participating in a raid against the German coastal gun battery at Auderville near Cap de la Hague at the northwest tip of the Cotentin Peninsula.

OPPOSITE TOP: This memorable photograph, taken on Monday, June 5, 1944, shows a battered Boeing B-17 Flying Fortress from the 100th Bombardment Group (Heavy), Eighth Air Force during a bombing raid over the Forêt Domaniale d'Écault between the beachside communities of Équihen-Plage and Hardelot Plage in the department of Pas-de-Calais. The 2.5-mile-wide stretch of shoreline shown here is 5 miles south of the Gare Maritime on the waterfront in downtown Boulogne. Eighth Air Force heavy bombardment groups, such as the 100th, flew missions in support of the D-Day invasion before, on, and after June 6.

OPPOSITE BOTTOM: A Martin B-26 Marauder medium bomber from the U.S. Ninth Air Force departing its target area near the city of Caen on the afternoon of D-Day. The aircraft is in flight above the Queen sector of Sword Beach near the beachside community of Riva Bella with the traffic circle at the intersection of Avenue de Verdun and Boulevard de France visible at the bottom left.

LEFT: A B-26C-45 Marauder from the 386th Bombardment Group, 555th Bombardment Squadron in flight over the Forêt de Cerisy south of Le Molay-Littry near the village of Balleroy on D-Day. The billows of smoke are rising from bombed points along the road between Bayeux and Saint-Lô, which is now called D572. This spot is ten miles southwest of Bayeux and thirteen miles due south of the Normandy American Cemetery. On the far right, just above the rising clouds of smoke, the three parallel buildings of a farm located near Le Bas de Montfiquet can be seen.

ABOVE: Three U.S. glider pilots walk down the middle of a row of Airspeed Horsa gliders on June 5, 1944. Although it was a British-made aircraft, the Horsa was used in great numbers by the U.S. Army during the Normandy invasion because it offered greater carrying capacity.

BELOW: Men of the 307th Airborne Medical Company, 82nd Airborne Division walk out to the gliders at RAF Greenham Common (USAAF Station 486) on the Salisbury Plain in Berkshire during the afternoon of June 6, 1944. They are about to be flown to Landing Zone W two miles southeast of Sainte-Mère-Église near the village of Les Forges as part of Mission Elmira, the reinforcement of the 82nd Airborne. A C-47 Skytrain (s/n 43-15306) from the 88th Troop Carrier Squadron, 438th Troop Carrier Group, Ninth Air Force can be seen in the background.

TOP LEFT: Men of the 307th Airborne Medical Company, 82nd Airborne Division wait to board the Horsa glider that will take them to Normandy. They are wearing M1941 Field Jackets, M1937 Olive Drab Wool Field Trousers, Russet Service Shoes, and Leggings. Several 82nd Airborne Division shoulder patches can be clearly seen in the photograph. **TOP RIGHT:** Men of the 307th Airborne Medical Company and the Divisional Headquarters of the 82nd Airborne Division wait to board the Horsa glider that will take them to Normandy on June 6, 1944. One of the men on the left is holding a Graflex Speed Graphic camera. **RIGHT:** Men of the 325th Glider Infantry Regiment, 82nd Airborne Division wait for their flight to Normandy on June 6, 1944. An interesting assortment of weapons, equipment, and uniform items can be seen here: M1937 Olive Drab Wool Field Trousers, M1937 Olive Drab Flannel Shirts, M1941 Field Jackets, russet Service Shoes with leggings, B-4 Life Preservers, M1910 Entrenching Tools, and M3 Trench Knives in both the M8 Scabbard and the M6 Leather Sheath. Two men are carrying the M1 2.36-inch rocket launcher (or bazooka) while the rest all seem to be armed with the M1 Garand rifle. **RIGHT:** With their M1 rifles at stack arms, these 325th Glider Infantry Regiment troopers have assembled in front of the Airspeed Horsa gliders that will soon take them to Normandy. Many 82nd Airborne Division shoulder patches can be seen here, as well as B-4 Life Preservers and bandoliers of ammunition for their M1 Garand rifles. One gliderman in the background has shouldered an M1A1 2.36-inch Rocket Launcher. **RIGHT:** Two enlisted men and an officer from the 325th Glider Infantry Regiment climb aboard an Airspeed Horsa glider at their embarkation airfield shortly before D-Day. They are wearing M1937 Olive Drab Wool Field Trousers, M1941 Field Jackets, B-4 Life Preservers, and M1 Steel Helmets. The soldier entering the Horsa is carrying an M1 2.36-inch Rocket Launcher, he is wearing russet Type II service shoes with leggings, and (for some unknown reason) he has a GI spoon in his back left pocket. The man behind him carries an M1 Garand rifle and has an M1 Bayonet in an M7 Scabbard attached to his M1923 Dismounted Cartridge Belt. **RIGHT:** The troop compartment of an Airspeed Horsa glider is packed full of soldiers from the 325th Glider Infantry Regiment on June 6, 1944. The soldier with the glasses on the right is armed with an M1A1 Thompson Submachine Gun while the others are armed with the eight-shot, semiautomatic M1 Garand rifle.

The bold nose art of "Pelican Pappy," a veteran C-47 Skytrain from the 14th Troop Carrier Squadron, 61st Troop Carrier Group, Ninth Air Force Troop Carrier Command. On D-Day, this aircraft would carry paratroopers from the 507th Parachute Infantry Regiment, 82nd Airborne Division from the airfield at Barkston Heath near Grantham in Lincolnshire to Drop Zone T between Gourbesville and Amfreville in Normandy.

ABOVE: First Lieutenant Alex Bobuck of Headquarters 3rd Battalion, 506th Parachute Infantry Regiment, 101st Airborne Division is about to begin checking his men's equipment during a staged press event on June 4, 1944, on the airfield at Exeter in Devonshire. Behind them, "Lady Lillian," a C-47 from the 95th Troop Carrier Squadron, 440th Troop Carrier Group, serves as only a symbolic backdrop for the photograph because another aircraft would deliver these men to France on D-Day. **LEFT:** C-47 Skytrain transports from the 87th, 89th, and 90th Troop Carrier Squadrons, 438th Troop Carrier Group are parked on the tarmac at Greenham Common in Berkshire County alongside dozens of Airspeed Horsa gliders.

ABOVE: These paratroopers from the Headquarters 3rd Battalion, 506th Parachute Infantry Regiment, 101st Airborne Division are marching out to the C-47 that will take them to Normandy on the airfield at Exeter in Devonshire on Monday, June 5, 1944. **BELOW:** Paratroopers from the 2nd Battalion, 508th Parachute Infantry Regiment, 82nd Airborne Division perform equipment checks on their harnesses and T-5 parachutes on the embarkation airfield at Saltby in Leicestershire before departing for Normandy. Each man is wearing a reinforced M42 Jumpsuit, an 82nd Airborne Division patch on his left shoulder, and an American flag on his right shoulder.

TOP: A C-47 Skytrain (s/n 42-93096) shortly before departing for Normandy. This aircraft flew as Serial 5, Plane 17 on its first combat mission during the predawn hours of June 6, 1944, as part Operation Neptune/Overlord—the allied invasion of Normandy. As Chalk 17, this aircraft carried Pathfinder team two of the 508th Parachute Infantry Regiment, 82nd Airborne Division to Drop Zone N near Amfreville west of the village of Sainte-Mère-Église. **ABOVE LEFT:** General Eisenhower, Supreme Commander of the Allied Expeditionary Force, chats with paratroopers of E Company, 502nd Parachute Infantry Regiment, 101st Airborne Division at USAAF Station AAF-486/RAF Greenham Common in Berkshire on Monday, June 5, 1944. The trooper wearing the "23" placard around his neck is 1st Lt. Wallace C. Strobel of Saginaw, Michigan, and he has a British No. 75 Hawkins mine strapped to his left shin. *National Archives and Records Administration/US Army Signal Corps 111-SC-194399* **ABOVE RIGHT:** Another view of Ike at Greenham Common with the men of the 502nd Parachute Infantry Regiment. The naval officer in the background is Cmdr. Harry C. Butcher (U.S. Navy Reserve), General Eisenhower's naval aide from 1942 to 1945. *National Archives and Records Administration/US Army Signal Corps 111-SC-421508*

ABOVE LEFT: T-4 Joseph F. Gorenc of Headquarters Company, 3rd Battalion, 506th Parachute Infantry Regiment, 101st Airborne Division boards a C-47 Skytrain (s/n 42-92717) from the 98th Troop Carrier Squadron, 440th Troop Carrier Group, 50th Troop Carrier Wing at Exeter in Devon. *National Archives and Records Administration/US Army Signal Corps 111-SC-190367* **ABOVE RIGHT:** Paratroopers from F Company, 2nd Battalion, 506th Parachute Infantry Regiment, 101st Airborne Division await takeoff aboard a C-47 Skytrain from the 439th Troop Carrier Group on the airfield at Upottery in Devonshire. They are (from left to right): William G. Olanie, Frank D. Griffin, Robert J. Noody, and Lester T. Hegland. Noody is armed with the M1 2.36-inch Antitank Rocket Launcher, more popularly known as the Bazooka. **BELOW:** An unknown 82nd Airborne Division paratrooper who drowned in the inundated area of the Douve River near Beuzeville-la-Bastille after becoming hopelessly entangled in his parachute canopy and risers during the predawn hours of June 6, 1944. He was most likely a member of the 508th Parachute Infantry Regiment.

ABOVE LEFT: The wreckage of a troop carrier C-47 brought down by German antiaircraft fire during the predawn hours of Tuesday, June 6, 1944. **ABOVE RIGHT:** The wreckage of a C-47 Skytrain (s/n 42-100876) from the 93rd Troop Carrier Squadron, 439th Troop Carrier Group that crashed near L'Isle Marie, between Chef-du-Pont and Picauville, during the predawn hours of June 6, 1944. The aircraft took off from the airfield at Upottery in Devonshire during the night of June 5, 1944, and sortied for Normandy as Chalk 58/Serial 12 of Mission Albany—the predawn parachute combat assault of the 101st Airborne Division. During the final approach to the drop zone, s/n 42-100876 was struck by ground fire and began burning. The pilot, 2nd Lt. Marvin F. Muir, struggled to maintain control of the aircraft while the paratroopers completed their jump. In so doing, he sacrificed his life and the lives of his crew to save a stick of soldiers from the 506th Parachute Infantry Regiment. The U.S. Army posthumously awarded Second Lieutenant Muir the Distinguished Service Cross for the action. The other members of the crew who were lost in the crash were 2nd Lt. Kenneth C. Bell (Copilot), 2nd Lt. John A. Marisay (Navigator), Sgt. Phillip Snyder (Radio Operator), and Staff Sgt. Clifford L. Burgess (Crew Chief). **BELOW LEFT:** A British Airspeed Horsa glider—part of the USAAF's airborne operation—has come to rest in a Norman hedgerow with its cockpit projecting out over the Rue de Baudienville (D15) between Ravenoville and Sainte-Mère-Église. The glider's nose wheel broke away during the crash landing and ended up in the road. **BELOW RIGHT:** This tragic photograph shows the bodies of eight men from A Company, 325th Glider Infantry Regiment, 82nd Airborne Division who were killed when their glider crashed spectacularly at Holdy near Sainte-Marie-du-Mont shortly after daybreak on Wednesday, June 7, 1944 (D+1). The aircraft—Horsa LJ-135 from the 437th Troop Carrier Group based at Station USAAF-469/RAF Ramsbury in Wiltshire—sortied that night as part of Serial 34 of Mission Galveston. It was supposed to have landed on Landing Zone W near Les Forges, but instead it crashed, killing fourteen and injuring fifteen. *National Archives and Records Administration/US Army Signal Corps 111-SC-190474*

ABOVE: An Airspeed Horsa glider that has made a successful landing in Normandy, although it has suffered light damage to its right wingtip. The aircraft's tail has been removed to allow for the unloading of either a Jeep or an airborne 75mm howitzer using the ramps that are still present. Note that this Horsa bears the name "Kansas" near its nose and that its invasion stripes were not applied with great precision. **RIGHT:** Another USAAF Horsa glider that has suffered a violent crash-landing in Normandy. The British delivered 301 Horsas to the Ninth Air Force prior to the invasion. **OPPOSITE TOP:** An Airspeed Horsa glider numbered Chalk E1 provides shade for a group of grazing cows after its imperfect landing in Normandy. The number *401* may indicate that the aircraft carried elements of the 401st Glider Field Artillery Regiment. **OPPOSITE BOTTOM:** A U.S.-made Waco CG-4A glider that has suffered a destroyed nose section as a result of a rough landing in Normandy (despite the fact that it is equipped with the reinforced "Griswold nose"). Although the CG-4 glider was smaller than the British-made Horsa, more CG-4s participated in the Normandy invasion.

ABOVE: An Airspeed Horsa glider marked "R15" sits in a field near the intersection of D14 and D913 just northeast of Sainte-Marie-du-Mont after making a perfect, three-point landing after 9 p.m. on D-Day as part of Mission Keokuk. **OPPOSITE TOP LEFT:** This photograph powerfully illustrates just how dangerous Norman hedgerows could be to gliders. Shown here is what is left of a Waco CG-4A nicknamed "The Fighting Falcon" that landed on Landing Zone E two miles west of Sainte-Marie-du-Mont shortly before 4 a.m. on D-Day and then slammed into a hedgerow while still traveling more than fifty miles per hour. The crash killed the Assistant Division Commander of the 101st Airborne Division, Brig. Gen. Don F. Pratt, as well as the aircraft's copilot, Lt. John B. Butler, whose body can still be seen in the wreckage. The site of this crash is marked today by a memorial situated at the junction of D129 and D329 at the edge of the field where it happened 2 miles north of Saint-Côme-du-Mont and 3.5 miles southeast of Sainte-Mère-Église. **OPPOSITE TOP RIGHT:** The wreckage of another Ninth Air Force CG-4A Waco glider that has met its fate among Normandy's infamous hedgerows. The aircraft's tail number (318885) can be seen clearly in the wreckage, as well as its invasion stripes. **OPPOSITE BOTTOM:** Norman cows laze around Waco CG-4A glider s/n 42-77717, an aircraft that was Chalk 2, Serial 31 of Mission Elmira—the 82nd Airborne Division's glider operation on the evening of D-Day. This aircraft departed Greenham Common airfield in Berkshire on June 6, was towed across the English Channel by a C-47 from the 438th Troop Carrier Group, and subsequently landed safely on Landing Zone W at 9:20 p.m. with nine soldiers of the 82nd Reconnaissance Platoon. **RIGHT:** A portrait of 2nd Lt. Gayle R. Ammerman, taken while he was in training in the United States before being deployed overseas. On June 6, 1944, Ammerman was a pilot in the 81st Troop Carrier Squadron, 436th Troop Carrier Group of the Ninth Air Force's Troop Carrier Command, and he flew a British-made Airspeed Horsa glider to Landing Zone W near the villages of Sebéville and Les Forges south of Sainte-Mère-Église as part of Mission Elmira. *Courtesy of Dr. Gayle R. Ammerman*

LEFT: This famous photograph, taken at about 9 a.m. on June 7, shows a group of 101st Airborne Division paratroopers posing at Marmion Farm near Ravenoville, which is at the intersection of D14 and D15 four miles northeast of Sainte-Mère-Église and five miles north of Utah Beach. The men in the photograph are (from left to right): Pfc. Arthur A. Justice (B Company, 502nd Parachute Infantry), unknown, Pvt. Justo Correa (A Company, 506th Parachute Infantry), Pfc. Arthur J. Barker (B Company, 502nd Parachute Infantry), Pvt. Joe E. Ridgeway (B Company, 502nd Parachute Infantry), James Flanagan (C Company, 502nd Parachute Infantry, holding the flag), Pvt. Norwood B. Newinger (B Company, 502nd Parachute Infantry Regiment), Jerry Giarritano (with machete), Cpl. Earl H. Butz (Headquarters, 502nd Parachute Infantry), and Sgt. Smith C. Fuller (B Company, 502nd Parachute Infantry). There is a possibility that the man on the far right might be Albert Blithe (E Company, 506th Parachute Infantry Regiment), but this has not been proven to date. *National Archives and Records Administration/US Army Signal Corps 111-SC-189920* **ABOVE RIGHT:** The same spot at Marmion Farm remains virtually unchanged after seven decades.

LEFT: French civilians interacting with soldiers from 1st Battalion, 506th Parachute Infantry Regiment, 101st Airborne Division (including Headquarters Company personnel as well as paratroopers from A Company and C Company) on June 7, 1944, in front of the water pump at the intersection of Place de l'Église (D424) and Rue du Joly (D70) in the center of Sainte-Marie-du-Mont 3.5 miles west of Utah Beach. One of the French girls is Andree Dessolier, who was later married in a dress made of silk collected from U.S. equipment bundle parachutes. *National Archives and Records Administration/US Army Signal Corps 111-SC-190294*

ABOVE LEFT: Staff Sergeant Worster M. "Pappy" Morgan of Headquarters Company, 508th Parachute Infantry Regiment passes a Norman woman as he enters the village of Saint-Marcouf north of Utah Beach on June 6, 1944. He is armed with the M1A1 Thompson Submachine Gun, and the 82nd Airborne Division patch is clearly visible on his left shoulder. *National Archives and Records Administration/US Army Signal Corps 111-SC-190245* **ABOVE RIGHT:** A paratrooper from Headquarters Company, 508th Parachute Infantry Regiment, 82nd Airborne Division has just given two Norman children some chewing gum in the village of Saint-Marcouf north of Utah Beach on June 6, 1944. The presence of a rifle ammunition bandolier indicates that he is armed with the M1 Garand rifle. *National Archives and Records Administration/US Army Signal Corps 111-SC-189919*

ABOVE LEFT: This familiar image shows T-5 Donald J. MacLeod of Headquarters Company, 508th Parachute Infantry Regiment, 82nd Airborne Division and other paratroopers from his stick as they walk eastward down the Chemin des Azes in the village of Saint-Marcouf north of Utah Beach on June 6, 1944. The image is a frame taken from 35mm motion-picture film footage shot by T-4 Reuben A. Weiner of the 165th Signal Photographic Company, a Signal Corps photographer who jumped with the 508th on D-Day to document the airborne invasion. *National Archives and Records Administration/US Army Signal Corps 111-SC-189929* **ABOVE RIGHT:** The same group of men from Headquarters Company, 508th Parachute Infantry Regiment, 82nd Airborne Division is seen here a little farther down the Chemin des Azes near the church in Saint-Marcouf on June 6, 1944. This image is also a frame taken from the 35mm motion-picture footage T-4 Weiner filmed on D-Day. *National Archives and Records Administration/US Army Signal Corps 111-SC-189930*

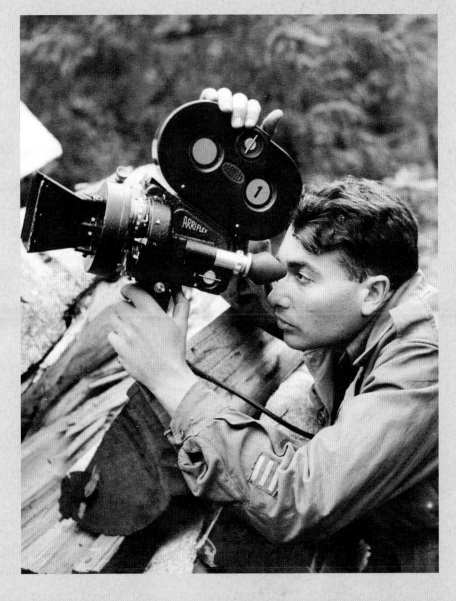

OPPOSITE TOP: T-4 Weiner from the 165th Signal Photographic Company also photographed the same Headquarters Company, 508th Parachute Infantry Regiment troopers as they took a rest break in front of the house at 3, Rue de la Fontaine in Ravenoville (a road now referred to as D14). They are Capt. Kenneth L. Johnson, Capt. Robert Abraham, Staff Sergeant Morgan, Pfc. Luther Marney Tillery, Pfc. Joel R. Lander, Pvt. John G. McCall, Pfc. James R. Kumler, and T-5 MacLeod.

OPPOSITE BOTTOM: The four photographers from the 165th Signal Photographic Company who jumped into Normandy with the 82nd Airborne Division: (left to right) T-4 Weiner, T-4 James L. "Jimmy" Bates, T-4 Joe Legault, and 1st Lt. Earl Witscher. Each man is equipped with the parachute and reserve necessary for the jump as well as the camera equipment he will use in France, which can be seen here carried in the padded bags strapped over each man's thighs. Each photographer also carried an M1911A1 .45-caliber Automatic Pistol. Because of lost and damaged gear, only Weiner would be able to record any images at all.

LEFT: T-4 Weiner of the 165th Signal Photographic Company films with an Arriflex camera at some point after his time in Normandy during the summer of 1944. On D-Day, he did not use this kind of motion-picture camera but rather a Bell & Howell 35mm Eyemo, as well as a Leica 35mm still camera.

LEFT: Many brothers fought on D-Day, but the story of what happened to Anthony J. Hitztaler (left) and his younger brother, William R. Hitztaler (right), is particularly intriguing yet tragic. At the time of the invasion, Tony was a private in the Headquarters Company of the 1st Battalion, 507th Parachute Infantry Regiment, 82nd Airborne Division, and Bill was a second lieutenant and pilot in the 14th Troop Carrier Squadron, 61st Troop Carrier Group. After a brief reunion at Barkston Heath airfield near Grantham in Lincolnshire, both men said their goodbyes and then took off for Normandy, where separate fates awaited them. Bill's aircraft (C-47 s/n 42-23638) was brought down by ground fire near the town of Negreville shortly after 2:20 a.m. on June 6, but he was able to parachute to safety and survive D-Day. Tony was not so lucky; he parachuted from another C-47 and landed safely, but his life ended violently before sunrise near a village named Hémevez.

ABOVE LEFT: The fourteenth-century church at Hémevez near Montebourg. This is where the bodies of seven paratroopers from the Headquarters Company of the 1st Battalion, 507th Parachute Infantry Regiment, 82nd Airborne Division were buried after being murdered by German soldiers during the predawn hours of Tuesday, June 6, 1944. Among the seven victims was Pvt. Tony Hitztaler. **ABOVE RIGHT:** On June 22, 1944, a U.S. Army Graves Registration Team came to the church cemetery at Hémevez to recover the bodies of the seven 507th paratroopers who were buried there after being murdered on D-Day. A Signal Corps motion-picture photographer filmed as the team exhumed the victims from the mass grave where they had been buried since June 6. Here, Tony Hitztaler's body is being lifted free of its first temporary grave.

Private John Katona of C Company, 507th Parachute Infantry is lifted from his temporary grave in the church cemetery at Hémevez on June 22, 1944.

The body of Private John Katona is seen here after being exhumed from his temporary grave in the church cemetery at Hémevez on June 22, 1944.

ABOVE LEFT: During the exhumation of the victims in the church cemetery at Hémevez on June 22, members of the Graves Registration Team conducted a careful search of each body and thoroughly documented wounds to collect evidence for an official investigation and an eventual war crimes trial. Here, Capt. Theodore F. Wright, U.S. Army Medical Corps, searches Private Katona's pockets immediately after his exhumation. **ABOVE:** Today, the church cemetery at Hémevez includes this simple memorial that remembers the seven 507th paratroopers who rested there temporarily after being brutally murdered on D-Day. They were Pfc. Daniel B. Tillman, Pvt. Robert G. Watson, Pvt. Robert E. Werner, Pvt. Delmar C. McElhaney, Pvt. Andrew W. Kling, Pfc. Elsworth M. Heck, and Pvt. Anthony J. Hitztaler. **LEFT:** After being exhumed from the church cemetery at Hémevez on June 22, 1944, Tony Hitztaler's body was moved to the temporary U.S. cemetery at Blosville south of Sainte-Mère-Église. Four years later, he was exhumed again and moved to the Normandy American Cemetery on Omaha Beach, where he is permanently buried in Plot B, Row 10, Grave 10.

ABOVE: An aerial view showing the crossroads town of Sainte-Mère-Église as a U.S. military convoy passes through it heading north. This town was of critical importance to the overall Normandy invasion plan because the network of roads leading to it and through it would provide for the circulation of vehicular traffic across the breadth and length of the Cotentin Peninsula. Of special significance was Route Nationale 13, which is the road running from the bottom to the top of this photograph. This road allowed rapid movement to the city of Carentan (just eight miles south) and to the port city of Cherbourg (just twenty miles northwest). The 505th Parachute Infantry Regiment of the 82nd Airborne Division was given the mission of capturing Sainte-Mère-Église before dawn on Tuesday, June 6, 1944. *National Archives and Records Administration/US Army Signal Corps 111-SC-199801* **OPPOSITE TOP LEFT:** Two German soldiers on a motorcycle pause for a photograph along Rue du Cap de Lainé (now

known as D974) in front of the Sainte-Mère-Église Hôtel de Ville (City Hall). During the German occupation from 1940 through 1944, the Hôtel de Ville was used as the Wehrmacht's District Civil Affairs Office. **OPPOSITE TOP RIGHT:** The Sainte-Mère-Église Hôtel de Ville has changed little since World War II. **OPPOSITE MIDDLE LEFT:** A group of German Army soldiers poses on the front steps of the Sainte-Mère-Église Hôtel de Ville during the German occupation. **OPPOSITE MIDDLE RIGHT:** The guard posts are gone now, and the front doors have been replaced, but the Sainte-Mère-Église Hôtel de Ville still looks very much as it did in the 1940s. **OPPOSITE BOTTOM LEFT:** A group of Luftwaffe troops poses on the front steps of the Sainte-Mère-Église Hôtel de Ville during the German occupation. **OPPOSITE BOTTOM RIGHT:** The flowers, the handrails, and the hedge are new, but otherwise the front steps to the Sainte-Mère-Église Hôtel de Ville look much the same as they did during the war.

ABOVE: German Army soldiers posing in front of a furniture shop on the Rue Géneral Kœnig near the Église Notre-Dame-de-l'Assomption in Sainte-Mère-Église during the occupation. The same location has changed little in more than seventy years.

ABOVE: German Army soldiers stand in formation on the southeast side of the Église Notre-Dame-de-l'Assomption in Sainte-Mère-Église during the occupation. **RIGHT:** Practically nothing has changed in more than seventy years.

ABOVE LEFT: A street scene along what is now known as Rue Général de Gaulle (D974) in the center of Sainte-Mère-Église on June 10, 1944. Before the construction of the bypass around the city, N-13 ran right through the center of the town. *Official U.S. Navy photograph now in the collections of the National Archives 80-G-252679* **ABOVE RIGHT:** In this June 10, 1944, view of Sainte-Mère-Église, the photographer was standing on the curb of what is now known as Voie de la Liberté (D974) looking north toward its intersection with what is now known as Rue de Verdun/Rue Division Leclerc (D15). To the left, La Fière and the Merderet River are just two miles away. To the right, the beach is just five miles distant. *Official U.S. Navy photograph taken by Combat Photo Unit Eight (CPU-8), now in the collections of the National Archives 80-G-252677* **BELOW LEFT:** Sergeant John P. Ray from Gretna, Louisiana, was a member of the stick of paratroopers from F Company, 505th Parachute Infantry Regiment, 82nd Airborne Division that came down in the middle of Sainte-Mère-Église at approximately 1:51 a.m. on June 6. He experienced a hard landing directly in front of the church and was still there struggling to free himself from his canopy and risers when a German soldier appeared and shot him in the stomach. That same soldier then spotted Pvt. Ken Russell and Pvt. John M. Steele suspended from the church itself. As he turned and prepared to shoot Russell and Steele, Sergeant Ray drew his M1911A1 .45-caliber Automatic Pistol and killed the German rifleman. Both

Russell and Steele survived the war, but Ray eventually succumbed to his wounds the next day. **BELOW RIGHT:** After his death in Sainte-Mère-Église, Sergeant Ray was initially buried in the temporary U.S. cemetery at Blosville near Les Forges. His remains rested there until 1948 when they were exhumed and moved to the cemetery on Omaha Beach for temporary reburial. Ray's young widow then chose to have him permanently buried in France—the place where he fought briefly and died in 1944. He now rests in Plot E, Row 26, Grave 36 of the Normandy American Cemetery. *Courtesy of Bryan Perissutti*

ABOVE LEFT: Two U.S. paratroopers from the 82nd Airborne Division trot northward on the Rue du Cap de Lainé (now known as D974) in Sainte-Mère-Église on Wednesday, June 7, 1944. After being misdropped on D-Day, they commandeered horses to help get them to their assigned assembly point. *National Archives and Records Administration/US Army Signal Corps 111-SC-190123* **ABOVE RIGHT:** One of the 82nd Airborne Division paratroopers from the previous photograph is seen here on horseback in the center of the intersection of the Rue du Cap de Lainé (now known as D974) and the Rue de Verdun/Rue Division Leclerc (D15) in Sainte-Mère-Église on Wednesday, June 7, 1944. The sign over his right shoulder indicates that the beach is only six miles away. *National Archives and Records Administration/US Army Signal Corps 111-SC-190326*

ABOVE LEFT: A MIAG-built Sturmgeschütz 40 Ausführung G (Sonderkraftfahrzeug 142/1) from 2, Panzerjäger Abteilung 243 knocked out on the N-13 highway just north of Sainte-Mère-Église by Pvt. John E. Atchley of H Company, 505th Parachute Infantry Regiment, 82nd Airborne Division on June 7, 1944. Although the road approaching the town's northern outskirts was covered by an M1 57mm Antitank Gun, the entire crew manning it became casualties during the German attack. As this StuG rolled forward unopposed, Private Atchley broke cover, ran to the gun, and proceeded to fire it by himself until the StuG was destroyed. At that point, the other vehicles in the German column turned and retreated. For singlehandedly stopping this attack, Atchley was subsequently awarded the Distinguished Service Cross. *National Archives and Records Administration/US Army Signal Corps 111-SC-190122* **ABOVE RIGHT:** Private First Class Clayton C. Hayes of F Company, 505th Infantry Regiment, 82nd Airborne Division helps Madame Digeon and Jacques Birette carry their luggage along the Route de Chef-du-Pont (D67) on the outskirts of Sainte-Mère-Église on June 8, 1944. Private First Class Hayes would be killed in Holland on September 20, 1944, during Operation Market Garden. *National Archives and Records Administration/US Army Signal Corps 111-SC-190287*

LEFT: Under the watchful eye of a paratrooper of the 101st Airborne Division, German prisoners dig trenches to protect the regimental command post of the 502nd Parachute Infantry, 101st Airborne Division at Les Mézières near Saint-Martin-de-Varreville. This sky soldier is armed with an M1A1 Thompson Submachine Gun, and he is also carrying two M3 fighting knives in M6 leather sheaths—one on his left calf, and the other on his belt. **BELOW:** C47s of the 96th Troop Carrier Squadron, 440th Troop Carrier Group, 50th Troop Carrier Wing fly over a U.S. Coast Guard–manned ship off of Utah Beach at low altitude. They are leaving the objective area after having flown Mission Memphis—the aerial resupply of the 101st Airborne Division on June 7, 1944. In this mission, sixty-three C-47s dropped 126,000 pounds of ammunition, 21,000 pounds of rations, and 42,000 pounds of other combat equipment. *U.S. Coast Guard photograph 26-G-2406*

ABOVE: A Douglas C-47 Skytrain (s/n 42-68840) tows a Waco CG-4A glider. The experience of flight in a CG-4A could be harrowing: "It gives a man religion," remembered Brigadier General James M. Gavin of the 82nd Airborne Division. **BELOW:** C-47s fly over Utah Beach on the morning of Wednesday, June 7, towing Airspeed Horsa gliders carrying reinforcements for the 82nd Airborne Division. These aircraft are from either Mission Galveston, which delivered eighteen Horsas, or from Mission Hackensack, which delivered twenty-five Horsas. Three military policemen, one of which is an NCO armed with an M1 Carbine, can be seen on the beach in the foreground. *National Archives and Records Administration/US Army Signal Corps 111-SC-190293*

C-47 Skytrain transport aircraft tow Waco CG-4A gliders to Normandy on June 7, 1944. Although the larger British Horsa glider offered greater carrying capacity, the CG-4A was nevertheless capable of hauling a 57mm antitank gun, a 75mm PAK Howitzer, a Jeep, or thirteen fully armed troops.

ABOVE: A USAAF Waco CG-4A glider landing on Advanced Landing Ground A-6 between La Londe and Beuzeville-au-Plain one mile northeast of Sainte-Mère-Église on June 11, 1944. The rolls of SMT at the left indicate the field is still under construction. By the time A-6 was ready for service, more than 2,500 rolls of SMT had been used. **RIGHT:** This hedgerow-enclosed Norman field near the village of Turqueville was used as a landing zone for seven Waco CG-4A gliders shortly after D-Day. Just 950 feet long and 320 feet wide (at the narrow part), its modest size illustrates how little space was required to land gliders. D67, also known as Rue du Jour J/Rue des Alliés, runs along the top border of the photo toward Sainte-Mère-Église, which is only 1.5 miles northwest. **OPPOSITE:** USAAF Douglas C-47 Skytrain transports bank for the return flight to England after their CG-4A gliders have cut loose from their towlines. Below them are the fields of Landing Zone W between Les Forges and Sébeville/Les Fontaines. The N-13 highway runs through the center of the image, Sainte-Mère-Église is just two miles away (to the left in the photograph), and Carentan is just five miles away (to the right). These aircraft constitute one of the serials of Mission Elmira, the airborne reinforcement of the 82nd Airborne Division on the evening of June 6, 1944.

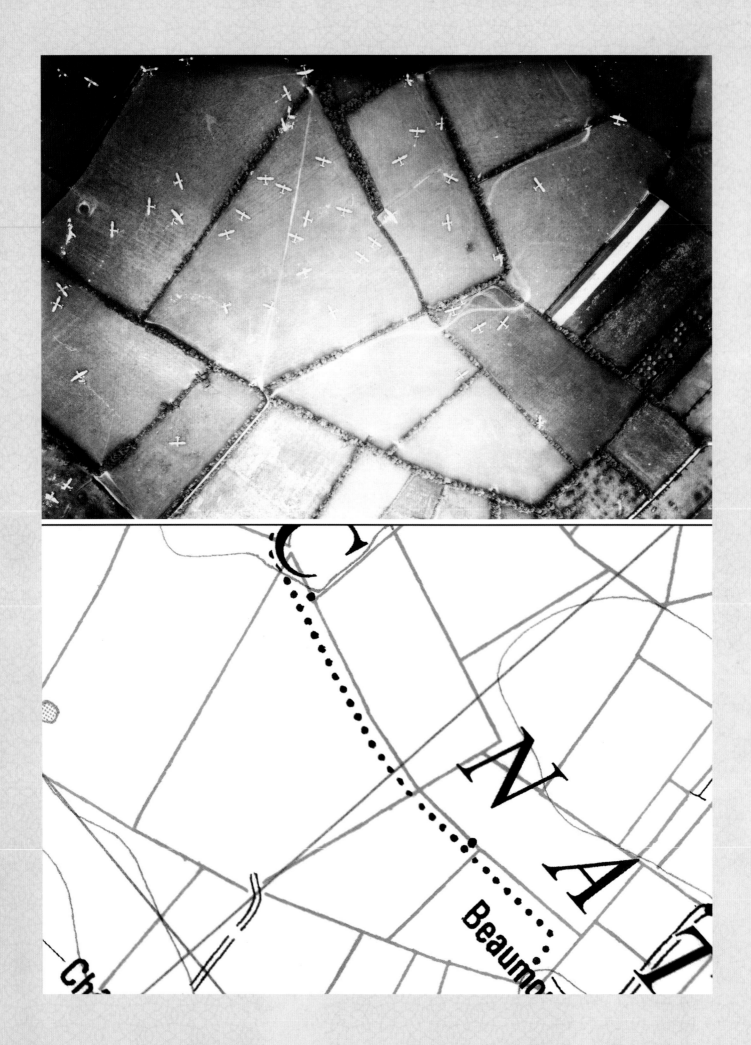

ABOVE LEFT: June 28, 1944: Three American paratroopers eat their first regular meal in seventeen days after successfully dodging German patrols following their landing near Cherbourg on D-Day. Their feet are swollen from wading through swamplands, but otherwise they are healthy. They hid during the daylight hours and traveled by night, reaching their outfit on the seventeenth day after their drop. Left to right: Pvt. Lawrence J. Davis of Trenton, Michigan; 1st Sgt. Fred G. Fitzgerald of Herrin, Illinois; and Sgt. Walter T. Murphy of Gloucester, Massachusetts. With them on the right is Capt. John D. Harrell from the 101st Airborne's divisional artillery. *National Archives and Records Administration/US Army Signal Corps 111-SC-324431* **ABOVE RIGHT:** Private John C. Rodrigues of Pawtucket, Rhode Island, gives two weary 82nd Airborne Division paratroopers their first taste of GI food in thirty-seven days. They were captured by the Germans during the latter part of D-Day, escaped after several days of imprisonment during a night march, and lived on raw potatoes most of the time. They finally contacted U.S. forces on July 15, 1944. In the center is Sgt. Robert D. Henderson of Seattle, Washington, and on the right is Sgt. Havrill W. Lazenby of Nashville, Tennessee. Both men were members of B Company, 505th Parachute Infantry Regiment, and both have armed themselves with captured weapons: Sergeant Henderson has a captured German Kar98k bolt-action rifle, and Sergeant Lazenby is carrying a Walther Gew41 semiautomatic rifle. *National Archives and Records Administration/US Army Signal Corps 111-SC-324432* **RIGHT:** A Lockheed P-38 Lightning fighter touches down on Emergency Landing Strip E-1, which was situated on the plateau between the Ruquet Valley and Saint-Laurent-sur-Mer on Omaha Beach. The aircraft on the right is a Piper Cub code L4 25 J, an artillery observation aircraft for the 2nd Infantry Division. This field was prepared by the 834th Engineer Aviation Battalion, and it opened at 6 p.m. on June 9, 1944. The airfield was abandoned on August 25, 1944. *National Archives and Records Administration/US Army Signal Corps 111-SC-190118* **OPPOSITE:** This photograph of Landing Zone W was taken shortly after D-Day and shows gliders that have landed in the hedgerow-enclosed fields immediately northwest of Chateau de Sébeville near Les Forges. The excerpt of the modern map below shows how the contours of those same hedgerows have remained almost unchanged for seventy years.

3

From the SEA

THE NAVAL ARMADA that would support the June 6 landings in Normandy was formidable. It would ultimately comprise nearly two hundred thousand seamen and merchant mariners from the Royal Navy, the Royal Canadian Navy, the French Navy, the U.S. Navy, the U.S. Coast Guard, the U.S. Merchant Marine, and other Allied navies. Almost seven thousand vessels, ranging in size from battleship to landing craft, would provide the transportation and the firepower for this impressive assembly of naval power. But the successful execution of such a vast and complex operation at sea would require expert coordination and extensive rehearsal. Thus, amphibious training exercises were a crucial part of the preparation for D-Day. Most of these rehearsals went off without major problems, but then in late April—just weeks before the invasion— one such exercise descended into disaster.

LEFT: A convoy of LCI(L)s sails across the English Channel toward the Normandy invasion beaches on D-Day, June 6, 1944. Each of these landing craft is towing a barrage balloon for protection against low-flying German aircraft. Among the LCI(L)s present are LCI(L)-56, at far left; LCI(L)-325; and LCI(L)-4. *U.S. Coast Guard Collection in the U.S. National Archives 26-G-2333*

ABOVE: LST-289 is seen here in port at Dartmouth in Devon after being severely damaged by a German E-boat torpedo attack off of Slapton Sands on April 28, 1944, during Exercise Tiger, a rehearsal for the Normandy invasion. BELOW: Close-up of the area of LST-289 showing the heavy damage she sustained during the E-boat attack in Lyme Bay. Thirteen men died in the upturned 40mm gun tub located on the ship's stern.

LCI Flotilla 10 is seen here departing Weymouth Bay in columns on Monday, June 5, 1944, for the voyage across the English Channel. At the center is LCI(L)-487, which is carrying 203 soldiers of the 18th Infantry Regiment, 1st Infantry Division (36 men from M Company, 18th Infantry and 167 men from K Company, 18th). This LCI would land on the Easy Red sector of Omaha Beach on D-Day, but it would not be able to use its stern anchor to winch itself back into deeper water. After spending twelve harrowing hours stranded under the German guns waiting for high tide, the heavily damaged landing craft would ultimately sail away under its own power.

Exercise Tiger

The practice invasion force arrived in its assembly area in Lyme Bay during the night of April 27, where it then dropped anchor just off Slapton on the Devon coast. The flotilla was Convoy T-4, and its purpose was to simulate the channel crossing for the upcoming Normandy landings. It consisted of eight LSTs (Landing Ship Tank) carrying vehicles and combat engineers of the 1st Engineer Special Brigade, a unit that would ultimately be part of Force U—the assembly of troops designated to land on Utah Beach on June 6. The LSTs were scheduled to conduct a practice landing at dawn on the 28th, but a flotilla of nine German high-speed torpedo boats known as E-boats from the Kriegsmarine base at Cherbourg intercepted them and carried out an attack using torpedoes and 20mm Oerlikon cannons. By the time the shooting ended, two LSTs had been sunk, two had been badly damaged and 749 soldiers and sailors had been killed. More men were lost during Tiger than would ultimately be lost in combat on Utah Beach on D-Day.

Despite the inauspicious prelude of Exercise Tiger, Operation Neptune put to sea shortly after General Eisenhower issued his famous "OK, let's go" order. From ports across southern England, the fleet weighed anchor and began to assemble into fifty-nine convoys for the voyage across the English Channel to the Baie de la Seine. Leading the way, the largest minesweeping operation in naval history created ten swept channels for the ships and landing craft to cross a waterway heavily sown with German anti-ship mines. The sealift represented by Neptune carried 130,000 Allied troops, 2,000 tanks, and 12,000 other vehicles. Although not the largest amphibious landing force in World War II history, it was the largest up to that time, and it was about to be put through hell.

No Such Thing as a Minor Wound

The U.S. Navy and the U.S. Coast Guard participated in the invasion as the Western Naval Task Force, subdivided into Force O landing on Omaha Beach and Force U landing on Utah Beach. Both forces fell under the command of Rear Adm. Alan G. Kirk, and they had to contend with rough seas, German coastal gun batteries, and the confusion that inevitably attends any major opposed amphibious landing operation. At dawn, the fire support group moved in and blasted targets ashore with everything from 5-inch to 14-inch fire while the transport group prepared the landing force that stormed ashore starting at 6:30 a.m. During this critical opening phase of the invasion, the landing craft that carried the troops to the beach took a great deal of punishment from anti-tank/anti-boat guns, mined beach obstacles, and machine-gun fire. When landing craft, infantry (LCI) (large)-85 approached Omaha Beach at 8:30 a.m. carrying engineers and military policemen, German shells and bullets swept over the open deck, killing fifteen and wounding thirty. In his after-action report, the landing craft's captain remembered, "There was no such thing as a minor wound." Obviously, sailors and Coast Guardsmen were in the line of fire on D-Day alongside the infantrymen, combat engineers, tankers, gunners, and Rangers.

LCIs from LCI Flotilla 10 passing the Jurassic Coast in Dorset as they depart for Normandy on Monday, June 5, 1944.

LEFT: *"You name it Boss, we'll hit it."*—An inscription chalked onto the top of Turret Two of the battleship USS *Arkansas* (BB-33). Written atop the turret's 12-inch/50-caliber gun barrels are the words (left) *Hitler's* and (right) *Downfall*, which indicate the confidence the crew felt in their gunnery. Also visible here are two lookouts with binoculars by the rangefinder at the right, crewmen's working jackets with hoods, and men limbering up with a medicine ball beside Turret One. *Official U.S. Navy photograph, now in the collections of the National Archives 80-G-244214* **BELOW:** The 14-inch/45-caliber main battery of the battleship USS *Nevada* (BB-36) in action against H.K.B. Azeville/Stützpunkt 133 (the German Army coastal gun battery at Azeville near Utah Beach) on the morning of June 6, 1944. Despite being heavily damaged on December 7, 1941, the *Nevada* was subsequently repaired and fit to fight on D-Day. *Official U.S. Navy photograph, now in the collections of the National Archives 80-G-252412*

ABOVE: Empty 5-inch shell casings litter the deck of the battleship USS *Nevada* (BB-36) on June 6. In addition to her fourteen-inch main battery, *Nevada* was armed with eight 5-inch/38-caliber guns in four Mk 28 Model 2 turrets. Also visible in this shot is one of the ship's quad 40mm Bofors gun tubs. As one of the most powerful warships of the Western Naval Task Force Fire Support Group, *Nevada* directed overwhelming firepower against German positions ashore on D-Day. **OPPOSITE TOP:** The battleship USS *Nevada* (BB-36) bombards German positions near Utah Beach in support of the landing of Force U on June 6, 1944. This photograph was taken from the *Baltimore*-class heavy cruiser USS *Quincy* (CA-71). *Official U.S. Navy photograph, now in the collections of the National Archives 80-G-231961* **OPPOSITE BOTTOM:** A German shell explodes close in to Île du Large, one of the two islands of the Îles Saint-Marcouf group. Sitting just 4.5 miles off of Utah Beach, the French fortified these islands at the beginning of the nineteenth century and militarily occupied them thereafter. Out of concern that the Germans were using the fortifications on the islands as observation posts, U.S. Army soldiers from the 4th and 24th Squadrons, 4th Cavalry Group occupied them before dawn on D-Day. This photograph was taken from the deck of the *Baltimore*-class heavy cruiser USS *Quincy* (CA-71) on June 6, 1944. *Official U.S. Navy photograph, now in the collections of the National Archives 80-G-231643*

RIGHT: The crew of a 20mm Oerlikon antiaircraft gun on LCI(L)-322 firing at targets ashore as it approaches the invasion beach. A U.S. Coast Guard landing craft, the 322 departed Salcombe in Devon on June 5 and landed troops on Utah Beach on the morning of June 6, 1944.

BELOW: U.S. Army soldiers inspect one of the casemates of Marine Küsten Batterie "Marcouf" (or Naval Coastal Battery Marcouf) in late June 1944. The only heavy battery on the east coast of the Cotentin Peninsula, Crisbecq was equipped with three Czechoslovakian Škoda 210mm (8.27-inch) guns, one of which can be seen in this photograph. These guns could cover the entire coastal area between Saint-Vaast-la-Hougue (seven miles northeast) and Pointe du Hoc (fifteen miles southeast). *National Archives and Records Administration 111-SC-190388.* **INSET:** A close-up of one of the Czechoslovakian Škoda 210mm (8.27-inch) guns of the Crisbecq Battery. This battery began firing at 6 a.m. on D-Day and was responsible for sinking the *Gleaves*-class destroyer USS *Corry* (DD-463) soon thereafter.

This casemate at the Crisbecq Battery does not look today (bottom) quite as it did in 1944 (top). As can clearly be seen in the modern photograph, it has sustained significant damage, mainly to its roof. However, this damage was not from battle; it was the result of an attempt to demolish the structure after the end of the Normandy campaign. The Škoda 210mm guns are long gone after having been scrapped at the end of the war. What appears to be a gun barrel is actually a section of pipe intended to give the impression that the casemate is armed. *National Archives and Records Administration 111-SC-190509*

ABOVE: The *Allen M. Sumner*–class destroyer USS *Meredith* (DD-726) had been in service for less than three months when she sailed as part of the Western Naval Task Force in June 1944. On the morning of June 6, *Meredith* was assigned to the fire support area off of Utah Beach, at which point she fired her first shots in anger. **OPPOSITE TOP:** While patrolling the waters five miles north of Îles Saint-Marcouf after midnight on June 7, USS *Meredith* (DD-726) was struck by a mine on the port side of her keel directly under fireroom number two. The ship immediately lost power and developed a twelve-degree list to starboard but did not sink. Just after 6 a.m., *Meredith* was towed to the advanced transport area north of Utah Beach, where efforts began to save the ship. Early in the morning on June 9, though, German aircraft approached that area, and a two-thousand-pound bomb landed about five hundred yards off the ship's bow. Shortly thereafter, *Meredith* broke in two. **OPPOSITE BOTTOM:** According to Cmdr. George Knuepfer, the *Meredith*'s commanding officer, at about 10 a.m. on June 9, the ship "suddenly gave a terrific crunch and broke in two." Thirty-two hours after the mine explosion that began the ordeal, the *Meredith* sank below the waves of the Baie de la Seine.

ABOVE: Soldiers from the 4th Infantry Division and the 101st Airborne Division packed aboard an LCT on the way to Utah Beach on the afternoon of June 6, 1944. Most of the troops here are wearing the M42 HBT fatigue uniform over their wool shirts and trousers, and a number of M1928 Haversacks are in evidence. The 101st Airborne Division trooper at the left facing the camera is wearing a U.S. Navy Inflatable Invasion Lifebelt and the M7 Assault Gas Mask Bag (worn on his chest), and a 101st Airborne patch can be seen on the left shoulder of his M1941 Field Jacket. The piece of equipment that the men are looking down to the right is an M3A4 Hand Cart carrying a T91E3/M63 Antiaircraft Mount for the Browning M2HB .50-caliber Machine Gun. *Official U.S. Navy photograph, now in the collections of the National Archives 80-G-59422.* **OPPOSITE TOP:** A group of soldiers from the 1st Infantry Division assembled on the deck of a transport preparing to go ashore on D-Day. A fascinating assortment of weapons and equipment can be seen here: M1928 Haversacks, assault vests, M7 Assault Gas Mask Bags, M1910 "T-handle" Entrenching Tools, M1943 Folding Entrenching Tools, and U.S. Navy inflatable lifebelts, some of which have been attached to equipment. The packboard at the lower right has twelve cardboard transport tubes tied to it containing M9A1 Antitank Rifle Grenades. Perhaps the most interesting detail in this photograph is the presence of almost twenty M1903 bolt-action rifles, many of which are protected by Pliofilm bags. *U.S. Coast Guard Collection in the U.S. National Archives 26-G-2336.* **OPPOSITE BOTTOM:** A boat team from the 16th Infantry Regiment, 1st Infantry Division loading onto a Higgins LCVP at the rail of the U.S. Coast Guard's *Arthur Middleton*–class attack transport USS *Samuel Chase* (APA-26). The troops are wearing M1928 Haversacks, canvas assault vests, M7 Assault Gas Mask Bags, and M1943 Folding Entrenching Tools, among other items. The soldier at the far right is armed with an M1903 Rifle and is handing a heavily laden packboard to one of the men already on the Higgins boat. *U.S. Coast Guard Collection in the U.S. National Archives 26-G-2338*

A group of soldiers from the 359th Infantry Regiment, 90th Infantry Division bound for Utah Beach on LCI(L)-326 on D-Day afternoon. The man in the front is carrying his M1 Garand rifle packed in a Pliofilm bag to protect it from sand during the landing, and he carries an 81mm mortar round in its cardboard transport tube threaded through the chest straps of his M1928 Haversack. A U.S. Coast Guard–manned landing craft, the 326 was built by Brown Shipbuilding Corporation in Houston, Texas, in 1942. *U.S. Coast Guard Collection in the U.S. National Archives 26-G-2402*

Men of the 359th Infantry Regiment, 90th Infantry Division transfer from LCI(L)-326 to a waiting Higgins boat on the afternoon of D-Day. Îles Saint-Marcouf can be seen in the background behind another group of LCIs, each of which trails an antiaircraft barrage balloon. *U.S. Coast Guard Collection in the U.S. National Archives 26-G-2408*

An LCT (Mark 6) packed full of men about to make the run into Utah Beach on the afternoon of June 6. They transferred to the LCT from the Coast Guard attack transport the photographer is on. The Jeeps are from the 4th Infantry Division, and, based on helmet markings, some of these men are from the 1st Engineer Special Brigade. *U.S. Coast Guard Collection in the U.S. National Archives 26-G-2380*

ABOVE: The *Northampton*-class heavy cruiser USS *Augusta* (CL-31) dominates the background of this photograph while LCVPs from the *Elizabeth C. Stanton*–class transport USS *Anne Arundel* (AP-76) pass in the foreground on their way to Omaha Beach carrying men of the 2nd Battalion, 18th Infantry Regiment, 1st Infantry Division. Lieutenant General Omar N. Bradley, commanding the U.S. First Army, and his staff embarked aboard *Augusta* for the landings in Normandy. *Official U.S. Navy photograph, now in the collections of the National Archives 80-G-45720* **BELOW:** LCVPs approach Omaha Beach on the morning of June 6, 1944.

RIGHT: This photograph shows LCVP PA26-15 from the U.S. Coast Guard attack transport USS *Samuel Chase* (APA-26) as it approaches the Easy Red sector of Omaha Beach (La Vallée du Ruquet) at approximately 7 a.m. on D-Day. Moments before, a German bullet set off a smoke grenade inside the vessel that then started a fire that caused the large plume of smoke seen here. After discharging his load of troops, the boat's coxswain, Coastguardsman Delba L. Nivens of Amarillo, Texas, his engineman, and his bowman put out the fire and returned to their transport. In the background, beach obstacles can be seen as well as troops seeking cover from enemy fire. *U.S. Coast Guard Collection in the U.S. National Archives 26-G-2342* **BELOW:** A U.S. Coast Guard coxswain named "Jim" is at the helm of an LCVP carrying troops from the 4th Infantry Division toward Utah Beach on D-Day. Two M1919A4 .30-caliber Machine Guns can be seen mounted in the gun tubs at the stern of the landing craft. *U.S. Coast Guard Collection in the U.S. National Archives 26-G-2349*

LCVPs from the Coast Guard attack transport USS *Samuel Chase* (APA-26) land assault troops from the 16th Infantry Regiment, 1st Infantry Division on the Easy Red sector of Omaha Beach on D-Day morning. The area in the background is the stretch of bluff between Exit E-1/Widerstandsnest 64 and Exit E-3/Widerstandsnest 62. After the war, the Normandy American Cemetery would ultimately be established on top of the plateau seen here. *U.S. Coast Guard Collection in the U.S. National Archives 26-G-2337*

ABOVE: The *Gleaves*-class destroyer USS *Harding* (DD-625) close to the Dog White sector of Omaha Beach on D-Day morning. La Grand Villa Hardelay (at 90, Boulevard de Cauvigny) is visible at the far right. Direct naval gunfire support from destroyers was decisive in determining the outcome of the fight at Omaha Beach. **OPPOSITE TOP:** This famous photograph, taken by Coast Guard Chief Photographer's Mate Robert F. Sargent, shows an assault boat team from E Company, 16th Infantry Regiment, 1st Infantry Division on an LCVP from the Coast Guard attack transport USS *Samuel Chase* (APA-26) as it approaches the Easy Red sector of Omaha Beach on D-Day morning. Among the equipment seen here are M1928 Haversacks, M1943 Folding Entrenching Tools, U.S. Navy inflatable lifebelts, and M1 Garand rifles protected by Pliofilm bags. The vertical stripes on the backs of the helmets of both the soldier looking over the top of the ramp and the soldier in the foreground indicate they are officers. *U.S. Coast Guard Collection in the U.S. National Archives 26-G-2340* **OPPOSITE BOTTOM:** In what has become one of the most famous photographs of D-Day, Chief Photographer's Mate Sargent captures the men of the same assault boat team seen in the previous photograph as they wade through the surf in front of the Easy Red sector of Omaha Beach at approximately 7:30 a.m. on June 6, 1944. These E Company, 16th Infantry Regiment troops are assaulting the area between Exit E-1 and Exit E-3 under fire from Widerstandsnest 62 and Widerstandsnest 65. On the beach directly ahead of the ramp can be seen M4 Sherman tank Number 9 from A Company, 741st Tank Battalion. *U.S. Coast Guard Collection in the U.S. National Archives 26-G-2343* **BELOW:** A U.S. Coast Guard LCM(3) brings wounded U.S. soldiers out to a transport for evacuation from the combat zone on D-Day. *U.S. Coast Guard Collection in the U.S. National Archives 26-G-2386*

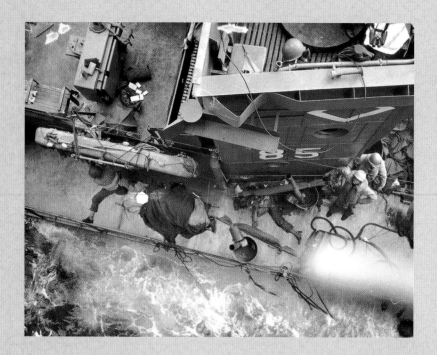 

ABOVE LEFT: In just a few minutes on Omaha Beach, LCI(L)-85 triggered a Teller mine under her bow and was then struck by twenty-five shells. The resulting damage was severe: fires started in troop compartments 1, 2, and 3, and water began to flood the forward part of the ship through holes that had been opened below the waterline by the explosion of the mine. The bodies of fifteen dead and thirty wounded littered the deck as the LCI(L)-85 withdrew to the transport area ten miles offshore. This photo reveals the grim scene waiting when the landing craft pulled alongside the USS *Samuel Chase* (APA-26) around noon. Note the casualties on deck, including a man on a stretcher (left center) whose face has been obscured by censors. Also note the binoculars atop a chart in the LCI(L)'s conning tower (upper right) and the life raft (at left) with paddles secured to its side. *U.S. Coast Guard Collection in the U.S. National Archives 26-G-2344* **ABOVE RIGHT:** Another view of the mortally wounded LCI(L)-85 alongside the USS *Samuel Chase* (APA-26) around midday on June 6. The dead from her earlier attempt to land on Omaha Beach have either been covered with blankets or pushed out of the way as the surviving crewmembers attempt to transfer everyone off of the foundering landing craft. On the bulkhead below and to the right of LCI(L)-85 are placards that read *Sicily* and *Italy*, identifying the 85 as a combat veteran of Operations Husky and Avalanche in 1943. Despite efforts to save her, LCI(L)-85 ultimately sank ten miles north of Omaha Beach at 2:30 p.m. on D-Day. *U.S. Coast Guard Collection in the U.S. National Archives 26-G-2350* **BELOW:** Although this familiar photograph is usually captioned as having been taken just off of Utah Beach on June 6, it actually shows pre-D-Day embarkation at Portland in Dorset on June 4. Some of the dead giveaways are the calm sea conditions, the shipboard life preservers being used by the troops instead of U.S. Navy inflatable lifebelts, and the Navy Dixie cup–

style caps being worn instead of helmets by some of the sailors. The fact that both LCVPs have only one machine gun mounted in their stern gun tubs, and that no gunners are manning these positions, clearly indicates these men are not in combat. The landing craft closest to the camera, LCVP PA13-22, is from the *Harris*-class attack transport USS *Joseph T. Dickman* (APA-13), a ship that would land elements of the 4th Infantry Division on Utah Beach on June 6. In the center background, LCI(L)-489 loads out alongside Rhino barge (RB)-24, which carries a load of Dodge WC54 3/4-ton ambulances. *U.S. Coast Guard Collection in the U.S. National Archives 26-G-2414*

Listing quite seriously to starboard, the Coast Guard–manned LCI(L)-85 is seen here at about noon on D-Day after having sustained heavy damage that morning on Omaha Beach. Troops from the 5th or 6th Engineer Special Brigade—including some military policemen, who could not be landed during the morning attempt—now line the rails preparing to be evacuated to the Coast Guard attack transport USS *Samuel Chase* (APA-26). LCI(L)-85 made her D-Day landing attempt at 8:30 a.m. on the border between Easy Red and Fox Green in front of the Widerstandsnest 62 bunker complex but was immediately raked by withering German fire. The landing craft's captain later described the scene with these words: "The 88s began hitting the ship; they tore into the compartments and exploded on the exposed deck. Machine guns opened up. Men were hit and men were mutilated. There was no such thing as a minor wound." *U.S. Coast Guard Collection in the U.S. National Archives 26-G-0610443*

ABOVE: This photo, which is also all too often mistakenly captioned as being in Normandy, shows a Rhino ferry full of Jeeps and GMC CCKW 2.5-ton cargo trucks in Lyme Bay off the coast of Devon. A VLA antiaircraft balloon is suspended above the ferry to protect it from strafing attack. **RIGHT:** An African-American soldier from an amphibian trucking company behind the wheel of a DUKW at sea. This six-wheel-drive amphibious truck, nicknamed the "Duck" by the GIs, provided a ship-to-shore capability that was critical during amphibious landings. In the aftermath of Operation Neptune, one officer described the DUKW as "worth its weight in gold." The U.S. Army was a segregated fighting force throughout World War II, and African-American troops were frequently assigned to support units like the quartermaster and amphibian trucking companies. **OPPOSITE TOP:** U.S. Coast Guard–manned LST-21 transfers supplies onto the Rhino that would ferry the load to the beach. This landing ship would support the initial British landings off of Gold Beach on June 6, 1944, and thereafter continue to supply Allied forces along the Normandy coast. *U.S. Coast Guard Collection in the U.S. National Archives 26-G-2366* **OPPOSITE BOTTOM:** LST-325 (right) and LST-388 (left) unload on Utah Beach at low tide on June 12, 1944, with barrage balloons deployed overhead. This method of delivering cargo was critical during the opening days of the invasion while the two Mulberry temporary harbors were being assembled. Note the sand ramp that has been built to facilitate unloading through the bow doors at low tide. *Official U.S. Navy photograph, now in the collections of the National Archives 80-G-252796*

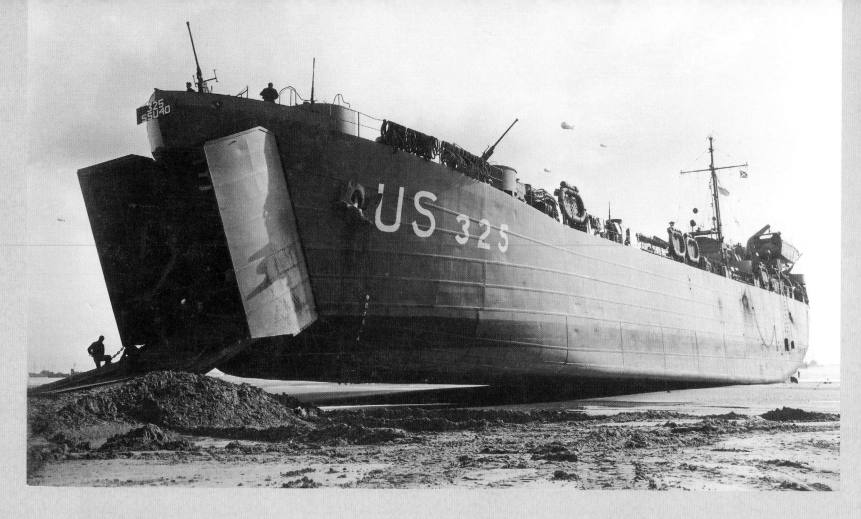

ABOVE: LST-325 sits high and dry on Utah Beach on Monday, June 12, 1944. In this photo, it is easy to see the roll-on/roll-off capability that made the LST such a versatile and effective weapon. LST-325 survived the war and was ultimately given to the Hellenic Navy in 1964. In early 2001, the ship returned to the United States and is now the USS LST Ship Memorial Museum in Evansville, Indiana. *Official U.S. Navy photograph, now in the collections of the National Archives 80-G-252795* **BELOW:** LST-325 (left) and LST-388 (right) are beached at low tide during resupply operations on Utah Beach on June 12, 1944. Visible here are four of the ship's 40mm antiaircraft guns and one of her LCVPs suspended from its lifting davits. *Official U.S. Navy photograph, now in the collections of the National Archives 80-G-252799*

ABOVE: LST-325 (left) and LST-388 (right) unload while stranded at low tide during resupply operations on June 12, 1944. Among the interesting things that can be seen in this photograph are a barrage balloon, LST-325's propellers, her rudders, and a "Danforth"-style kedge anchor hanging by a cable from her stern. *Official U.S. Navy photograph, now in the collections of the National Archives 80-G-252797*

BELOW: For the U.S. Navy, the excitement did not end on D-Day. Rather, it continued for quite some time thereafter as ships continued to provide naval gunfire support for the troops ashore pushing toward Cherbourg. In this dramatic photograph, a German 240mm coast artillery shell falls between USS *Texas* (BB-35), in the background, and USS *Arkansas* (BB-33) while the two battleships are engaging M.K.B. Hamburg/Stützpunkt 234 near Fermanville on June 25, 1944. Although Battery Hamburg was armed with the largest guns on the Cotentin Peninsula, it was still under construction when the invasion began. Despite this disadvantage, the battery managed to score two hits on *Texas*, wounding eleven men and killing one (a helmsman by the name of Christen Christensen). *Official U.S. Navy photograph, now in the collections of the National Archives 80-G-244210*

On the BEACHES

Omaha

The U.S. Army's V Corps, consisting of over forty thousand men (primarily from the 1st and 29th Infantry Divisions), was given the mission of landing on a 4.5-mile-wide stretch of beach between Vierville-sur-Mer and Grand Hameau. Here, they faced a series of strongpoints, fighting positions, and bunker complexes manned by approximately eight thousand German soldiers from the 352 and the 716 Infanterie Divisions. To make matters even more challenging, tall bluffs behind the dunes dominated the beach environment and presented the attackers with an intimidating terrain obstacle. When preliminary naval and aerial bombardments were largely ineffective at weakening the German defenses, the assault landing forces suffered high casualties, particularly in the Dog Green sector at Vierville-sur-Mer. Modest gains were made at certain points along the beach early in the battle, but it was not until several U.S. Navy destroyers came in close to provide direct naval gunfire support that the German defensive line began to crumble and U.S. troops were able to advance beyond the beachhead. Most of the German static defenses had been overcome by the afternoon, and elements of V Corps were able to begin their advance into the interior. In the end, almost one thousand U.S. Army soldiers were killed fighting the battle of Omaha Beach, making it the costliest beach of the five assaulted on June 6.

LEFT: Troops from the 5th Engineer Special Brigade wade through the surf in front of the Fox Green sector of Omaha Beach. These men are carrying M2HB .50-caliber machine guns and all of the equipment associated with them. One man carries the weapon's M3 tripod tied to a U.S. Navy M1926 Inflatable Lifebelt while the man closest to the camera carries an M17 Ammunition Chest that contains linked .50-caliber cartridges, also attached to a lifebelt. *National Archives and Records Administration/US Army Signal Corps 111-SC-190248*

ABOVE: LCI(L)-490 and LCI(L)-496 approach the area of Omaha Beach where the Easy Red sector (right) and the Fox Green sector (left) meet. These two landing craft are carrying elements of the 1st Infantry Division's 18th Infantry Regiment. In the background, smoke can be seen rising from the E-3 Draw at Colleville-sur-Mer. *National Archives and Records Administration/US Army Signal Corps 111-SC-189987* **BELOW:** LCI(L)-553 and LCI(L)-410 land troops on Omaha Beach during the initial assault on June 6, 1944, as seen from the conning station of LCI(L)-412. After being struck by two shells, LCI(L)-553 was left a wreck on the beach. *U.S. Navy photograph, now in the collections of the National Archives 80-G-421287*

These *holzfählen* (wooden stakes) were placed at an angle facing away from the beach and typically had an antitank Teller mine 42 on the end designed to explode on contact with a landing craft. Although the Germans placed many thousands of these obstacles along the coast of occupied France, the *holzfählen* seen here are located on the beach in front of Widerstandsnest 81 at Grandcamp-Maisy, three miles west of Pointe du Hoc. This position was armed with four machine guns, three 50mm antitank guns, and a tank turret mounted on a concrete base.

ABOVE: A view from just off of the Fox Green sector of Omaha Beach showing the two casemates of Widerstandsnest 62 and the E-3 Draw at Colleville-sur-Mer. A Duplex Drive Sherman medium tank from the 741st Tank Battalion sits at the water's edge, and *holzfählen* can be seen protruding above the surface of the water. **INSET:** A close-up shot of a *holzfähle* between Widerstandsnest 8 and Stützpunkt 9 in Dunes d'Audouville on Utah Beach. The Teller mine 42 on the tip of the obstacle is clearly visible here, as is one of the Type 677 casemates of Stützpunkt 9 (in the background on the left).

RIGHT: Born in Niederense in North Rhine–Westphalia in late 1925, Franz Gockel was conscripted into the German Army at the age of seventeen. He is seen here in September 1943 during basic training in Nijmegen in occupied Holland. **FAR RIGHT:** Gockel poses with a Gew98 Mauser rifle while training in Nijmegen in occupied Holland in late 1943. After basic training, he was transferred to occupied France and assigned to the

716 Infanterie Division. On June 6, 1944, Gockel was serving in Grenadier Regiment 726 at the Widerstandsnest 62 bunker complex looking down on the Fox Green sector of Omaha Beach.

Although the Third Reich produced outstanding automatic weapons before and during World War II, occasionally German troops were issued captured machine guns, such as the Polish Ckm wz.30 (seen in this photo). A water-cooled heavy machine gun chambered for the 7.92x57mm cartridge, the wz.30 was capable of laying down sustained bursts of fire in a way that air-cooled light machine guns simply could not. Gockel fired this type of weapon throughout the morning on D-Day until he was wounded and subsequently evacuated for medical treatment.

ABOVE: In this aerial view of Widerstandsnest 62, the two concrete casemates are clearly visible as well as some of the complex's ancillary fighting positions. The obelisk at the top of the hill above the upper casemate is the 1st Infantry Division Memorial. The white *X* at the left indicates Gockel's fighting position. **BELOW:** Three Sherman medium tanks from the 741st Tank Battalion on the shingle in front of the Easy Red sector of Omaha Beach on the morning of June 6. The tank on the left is a Duplex Drive Sherman from B Company, while the other two are regular Shermans from A Company that have had the deep-wading kit (sometimes referred to as the deep-water fording kit) installed.

These medics from the 5th Engineer Special Brigade are using the upper casemate of the Widerstandsnest 62 bunker complex as a base of operations. This casemate was armed with a Belgian 75mm FK 235(b) field gun on D-Day. The Germans captured a large number of these guns in 1940 and put them to use for training and as coastal artillery. The lower photograph shows the same casemate today with the 5th Engineer Special Brigade Memorial on its roof.

ABOVE: From the deck of a beached LCI, the same three 741st Tank Battalion Shermans can be seen from a much closer perspective. On the shingle at the far right is Sgt. James B. Larsen's deep-water-fording-kit Sherman from A Company, 741st, which is distinguished by the number *2* painted on the tank's engine exhaust funnel. Stuck in the sand at the center with several men sheltering from enemy fire behind it is Staff Sgt. Thomas R. Fair's fording-kit Sherman, also from A Company, 741st. Both of these vehicles made a direct landing on the beach from an LCT. Finally, on the shingle at the left is Staff Sgt. Turner G. Sheppard's Duplex-Drive Sherman from B Company, 741st—which was one of only two B Company Duplex Drive Shermans that managed to swim ashore on June 6. **BELOW** A view from the deck of the same LCI looking to the west down the length of the Easy Red sector of Omaha Beach on D-Day. This photograph was taken between the Ruquet Valley (Exit E-1) and the Colleville Draw (Exit D-3), and it shows two landing craft on the beach (an LCVP and an LCM-3), as well as a Jeep and a fording-kit Sherman tank on the shingle. Soldiers from E Company, 16th Infantry Regiment, 1st Infantry Division led by Lt. John M. Spalding used the demolished building in the center of the photograph as cover at about 7 a.m. on June 6.

ABOVE: This aerial reconnaissance photograph, taken on June 30, 1943, shows a small portion of what would ultimately become the Easy Red sector of Omaha Beach a little less than a year after it was taken. The demolished building that Lieutenant Spalding and men from E Company, 16th Infantry Regiment would use for cover on D-Day can be seen between the beach shingle and the bluff at the center of the image.

RIGHT: Near Widerstandsnest 60, elements of L Company, 16th Infantry Regiment, 1st Infantry Division have landed on the Fox Red sector of Omaha Beach protected from German fire by the area's high chalk cliffs. The two soldiers to the right wear 29th Infantry Division shoulder patches, which means they are from the four sections of E Company, 116th Infantry Regiment that washed up in this sector instead of Easy Green (where they were supposed to land). The man standing near the center has the stock of an M1A1 Carbine tucked under his left forearm while he cleans sand out of the weapon's action.

Soldiers belonging to the U.S. Army's V Corps approach the Easy Red sector of Omaha Beach on an LCVP on the afternoon of D-Day. The Ruquet Valley/Exit E-1 is visible on the right, and a group of DUKWs is clustered along the shingle at the left. Note the faint "No Smoking" sign on the LCVP's ramp and the interesting assortment of weapons being carried by the troops: six M1 Carbines, two M1 Garands, and a solitary M1903 rifle can be seen here. *National Archives and Records Administration 111-SC-320901*

ABOVE LEFT: Wounded men of the 3rd Battalion, 16th Infantry Regiment, 1st Infantry Division receive cigarettes and food at the 6th Naval Beach Battalion's medical aid station at the foot of the cliffs of the Fox Red sector of Omaha Beach on June 6. The soldier looking at the camera is twenty-two-year-old Nicholas A. Fina (s/n 12006788) of I Company, 16th Infantry Regiment. **ABOVE RIGHT:** Officers and men of C Company, 348th Engineer Combat Battalion rescue men of the 5th Engineer Special Brigade whose LCVP hit a mine and sank. *National Archives and Records Administration/US Army Signal Corps 111-SC-190366* **BELOW LEFT:** V Corps troops land from an LCVP on the Easy Red sector of Omaha Beach near the Ruquet Valley at about midday on June 6. On the beach are a DUKW amphibious truck and three M3 Half-tracks, two of which are towing M1 57mm antitank guns. Men can be seen moving up the bluff in the background as the 115th Infantry Regiment pushes south toward Saint-Laurent-sur-Mer, which was still held by the remnants of 716 Infanterie Division and 352 Infanterie Division. *National Archives and Records Administration/US Army Signal Corps 111-SC-190641* **BELOW RIGHT:** Combat engineers of the 5th Engineer Special Brigade come ashore on Omaha Beach at midday on June 6, 1944. They have just landed from LCT-538, a Mark 6 LCT built in late 1943 by Bison Shipbuilding Corporation in Buffalo, New York. The man bending over is armed with an M1 Garand equipped with the M7 Rifle Grenade Launcher. *National Archives and Records Administration/US Army Signal Corps 111-SC-189901*

ABOVE: High tide on Omaha Beach is seen here near Exit E-3 shortly before noon on D-Day. The LCVP at left center is from the *Arthur Middleton*–class attack transport USS *Samuel Chase* (APA-26), and the larger landing craft above it is LCI(L)-553, which delivered Company H, 115th Infantry Regiment, 29th Division to the beach before being damaged by enemy gunfire. Note the "Caution No Signal Left Drive" sign on the vehicle at the lower right and the DUKW on the beach at the far right. *National Archives and Records Administration/US Army Signal Corps 111-SC-189899* **BELOW:** Another view showing low tide on Omaha Beach after the start of the invasion, looking east toward the Easy Red, Fox Green, and Fox Red sectors. LCVPs, LCTs, DUKWs, and about twenty VLA barrage balloons can be seen here.

RIGHT: The Les Moulins Draw/Exit D-3 at the Easy Green sector of Omaha Beach is seen here at low tide after the invasion is well under way. Beached on the right is the U.S. Coast Guard's LCI(L)-87, the flagship of LCI Flotilla 10. This LCI was built by Brown Shipbuilding Corporation of Orange, Texas, in 1942 and 1943 and, by June 1944, was a veteran of amphibious landing operations in North Africa, Sicily, and Salerno, Italy. The prominent three-story house that can be seen on the left is Villa les Sables d'Or. This structure provided cover for a force of about fifty men under the command of Major Bingham, commander of the 2nd Battalion, 116th Infantry Regiment, making it possible for them to advance from the shingle to the mouth of the draw. **BELOW:** Exit D-3/ Les Moulins Draw at the Easy Green sector of Omaha Beach as seen from the air in June 2010. Although Villa les Sables d'Or is no longer there, and tour buses and cafés are now a permanent part of the scenery, this section of Saint-Laurent-sur-Mer still looks much as it did in 1944.

Not every vehicle made a perfect beach landing after D-Day. Here, a split-hatch M4 Sherman medium tank with appliqué armor nicknamed "DHOLE" (D 11) from D Company, 66th Armored Regiment, 2nd Armored Division sits swamped on Omaha Beach on June 10. The tank has the engine exhaust funnel from a deep-water fording kit in place, but there is no air intake funnel. Note the M2HB .50-caliber Machine Gun that has been dismounted and laid on top of the turret as well as the belt of .50-caliber cartridges sitting on top of the vehicle's engine deck.

Three U.S. Navy ensigns on Omaha Beach at low tide shortly after the invasion. They wear U.S. Navy rubberized parkas, M1 steel helmets, and flotation devices (two Kapok life preservers and one M1926 Inflatable Lifebelt).

RIGHT TOP: An M4 Sherman Medium Tank from G Company, 66th Armored Regiment, 2nd Armored Division drives off of the ramp of LST-281 on Omaha Beach at low tide on June 9, 1944. One of the ship's two LCVPs hangs from the starboard boat davits. **RIGHT MIDDLE:** Getting vehicles beyond the sandy beach was a problem invasion planners were fully aware of before D-Day. The difficulty associated with this critical moment of transitioning mechanized forces from landing craft and landing ships to dry land had already been experienced during training exercises in England. Here an M15A1 Combination Gun Motor Carriage from an antiaircraft battalion struggles through the sand after driving off of an LCT during a pre-invasion practice landing. With twin M2HB .50-caliber machine guns and the M1A2 37mm Autocannon, this half-track was not just a formidable antiaircraft weapon but also one that would contribute meaningfully to ground combat on Omaha Beach on D-Day. *National Archives and Records Administration/ US Army Signal Corps 111-SC-293770* **RIGHT BOTTOM:** The U.S. Coast Guard's LCI(L)-92 lies abandoned on the Dog Red sector of Omaha Beach. A few minutes after 8 a.m. on D-Day, she was approaching the beach with 192 soldiers aboard when German shells set her Number 1 troop compartment on fire. With the entire forward deck covered by burning fuel, and with machine gun fire raking her starboard side, the landing craft switched to portside unloading. When it was not possible for LCI(L)-92 to return to deep water, she was abandoned on the beach at 2 p.m., where she was still sitting when this photograph was taken several days later.

OPPOSITE: During the final run into the Easy Red sector of Omaha Beach on D-Day, LCT-25 struck an underwater obstacle that caused her engine room to flood. Since she could not return to deep water, the crew beached the landing craft under fire from German guns. Later in the day, German mortar rounds started a fire that burned the eleven vehicles on board. These burned vehicles, belonging to the 197th Anti-Aircraft Automatic Weapons Battalion, were still on the abandoned landing craft when the top photograph was taken several days later. The wreck of LCT-25 was still on Omaha Beach in August 1946 when a French family snapped the bottom photograph.

BELOW LEFT: LCT-603 is seen here landing Jeeps on the Fox Red sector of Omaha Beach later on D-Day morning. These vehicles are from various units assigned to the 1st Infantry Division: the 32nd Field Artillery Battalion, the 16th Infantry Regiment, the 18th Infantry Regiment, and the 81st Chemical Mortar Battalion. The three Jeeps still in the water have each been waterproofed in anticipation of this very moment. By the time this photograph was taken, LCT-603 had already made one trip to Omaha Beach after having delivered four Duplex Drive Shermans from B Company, 741st Tank Battalion earlier that morning. **BELOW RIGHT:** The scene on Omaha Beach soon after D-Day, showing stranded landing craft and piles of supplies. LCT-555 is in the center, with her stern toward the beach. Royal Navy LCT(A)(5)-2421 is beyond her, to the left, lying parallel to the beach. The closest vehicle in the photograph is a DUKW with the name *Angela* and the words *Cincinnati, Ohio* stenciled on its side. *U.S. Navy photograph, now in the collections of the US National Archives 80-G-252568* **BOTTOM LEFT:** African-American soldiers of the 320th Anti-Aircraft Barrage Balloon Battalion (VLA), First Army prepare to deploy their balloon on Omaha Beach during the Normandy invasion. The 320th was one of several African-American units that participated in the invasion. *National Archives and Records Administration/US Army Signal Corps 111-SC-191713* **BOTTOM RIGHT:** The antitank ditch near the Ruquet Valley/Exit E-1 on Omaha Beach, looking east. The ditch was fifteen feet from the high-water mark. There were antitank ditches on both sides of the Exit E-1 Draw, as well as at Les Moulins (Exit D-3) and in front of the Colleville Exit (E-3).

ABOVE: The 81st Chemical Mortar Battalion in action on the Fox Green sector of Omaha Beach in front of Widerstandsnest 61 on the afternoon of June 6. On the left, the crew of an M2 4.2-inch Mortar prepares to drop a round down the tube to fire it toward the Widerstandsnest 62 bunker complex, which is still held by the enemy. **LEFT:** One of the casemates of the Widerstandsnest 72 defensive complex at Vierville-sur-Mer on Omaha Beach's Dog Green sector. This structure faced eastward down the length of the beach and housed a lethal 5cm Panzerabwehrkanone 38 (L/60) antitank gun. *National Archives and Records Administration/US Army Signal Corps 111-SC-275820*

RIGHT: This view from inside the H677 casemate at Widerstandsnest 72 shows the superb field of fire its 8.8cm Panzerabwehrkanone 43/41 commanded over the Dog Green sector of Omaha Beach. The "corncob" blockships of "Gooseberry 2" for the American Mulberry Harbor can be seen in the background. *National Archives and Records Administration/US Army Signal Corps 111-SC-275816* **BELOW:** An aerial view of Exit D-1 at the Dog Green sector of Omaha Beach and the village of Vierville-sur-Mer taken in June 2010. With a gentle slope and a decent road, this draw allowed vehicular traffic to advance off the beach to the high ground above it. The heaviest casualties of the entire invasion were suffered here on the morning of June 6.

ABOVE LEFT: One of the more interesting defensive structures on Omaha Beach was this Panzerkampfwagen III turret mounted on an H246-type bunker at Widerstandsnest 68 near Saint-Laurent-sur-Mer. Armed with a 7.5cm gun, the position could direct fire across the Les Moulins Draw/Exit D-3 to protect what would ultimately become the Easy Green sector on June 6. **ABOVE RIGHT:** U.S. troops raise the American flag over the largest bunker of Widerstandsnest 61 on Omaha Beach shortly after D-Day. This H677-type casemate housed an 8.8cm Panzerabwehrkanone 43/41 that directed gunfire across the Fox Green and Easy Red sectors during the initial phase of the invasion and was turned into a medical aid station after its capture.

ABOVE LEFT: U.S. Army vehicles move inland using Exit E-1 at the Ruquet Valley on the Easy Red sector of Omaha Beach shortly after D-Day. Among the vehicles present are a DUKW amphibious truck (at right), a Jeep towing a Bantam T-3 Trailer, and a road grader. A VLA antiaircraft barrage balloon is suspended above the Widerstandsnest 65 bunker. The four M2HB .50-caliber Machine Guns of a Maxson M45 Quadmount on an M16 Multiple Gun Motor Carriage can be seen below and to the right of the barrage balloon. *U.S. Navy photograph, now in the collections of the US National Archives 80-G-252580* **ABOVE RIGHT:** A closer look at the Widerstandsnest 65 bunker shortly after D-Day when it housed the Provisional Engineer Special Brigade Group Headquarters. Officers and men of the 2nd Infantry Division chat with some of the engineers as a Dodge WC56 Command Car towing a Bantam T-3 Trailer passes. A sign marks the casemate as being part of the "Information Detachment," and a tarp has been spread over the battle-damaged concrete from D-Day. *U.S. Navy photograph, now in the collections of the US National Archives 80-G-252577*

ABOVE LEFT: A closer look at Widerstandsnest 65 and some of the officers and men of the Provisional Engineer Special Brigade Group Headquarters. Note that they have set up a dining room table in front of the casemate's embrasure and that they are using it as a field expedient information booth. The man at the far right is a photographer and is carrying a Bell & Howell Eyemo motion-picture camera in his left hand. *National Archives and Records Administration/US Army Signal Corps 111-SC-190266* **ABOVE RIGHT:** After the engineers set up shop inside Widerstandsnest 65, one soldier hung his M1938 Dispatch Case off of the muzzle of the 5cm Panzerabwehrkanone 38 (L/60) antitank gun arming the casemate. This weapon laid down devastating fire over the Ruquet Valley/Exit E-1 and the Easy Red sector of Omaha Beach on D-Day morning until the 467th Anti-Aircraft Automatic Weapons Battalion knocked it out. *U.S. Navy photograph, now in the collections of the US National Archives 80-G-252574* **BELOW:** Soldiers of the U.S. Army's 2nd Infantry Division climb the bluff above the Ruquet Valley on Wednesday, June 7, 1944, after having just landed on the Easy Red sector of Omaha Beach. It is noteworthy that most of the men seen in this photograph are armed with the .30-caliber M1903 bolt-action rifle and not the M1 Garand rifle. Below them can be seen the Widerstandsnest 65 bunker, which had been knocked out the day before by the men of the 467th Anti-Aircraft Automatic Weapons Battalion.

A view from the top of the bluff above Widerstandsnest 65 looking down on the Easy Red sector of Omaha Beach. L'Abri Côtier, the house in the center of the photograph, was used as an observation position by the Germans before the landings. Note the Dodge WC54 1/2-ton 4x4 Field Ambulance at the left and the wide variety of landing craft on the beach (including an LCI, an LCT, three LCMs, and three LCVPs). Six "corncob" blockships of "Gooseberry 2" for the American Mulberry Harbor can be seen in the background.

In this aerial view of the Ruquet Valley/Exit E-1, the Widerstandsnest 65 bunker can be seen at the center, and the westernmost corner of the Normandy American Cemetery can be seen at the top left.

FOLLOWING PAGES: A view of the Fox Green sector of Omaha Beach overlooking the E-3 beach exit as seen from Widerstandsnest 61 on (probably) June 9. In this photograph, ten LSTs are taking advantage of the low tide to land vehicles directly on the beach, as they would continue doing for several months to come. Among identifiable ships present are LST-532 (in the center of the view); LST-262 (the third LST from the right); LST-310 (the second LST from the right); LST-533 (partially visible on the far right); and LST-524. Note the abundance of barrage balloons overhead and the "half-track" convoy forming up on the beach. LST-262 was one of ten Coast Guard–manned LSTs that participated in the invasion. *U.S. Coast Guard Collection in the U.S. National Archives 26-G-2517*

Utah

The flanks of the invasion area became battlegrounds of pivotal importance during the initial phase of the Normandy battle. On the right flank, the west coast of the Cotentin Peninsula offered the Allies rapid access to the port city of Cherbourg, as well as maneuver space for the reinforcing units needed for the drive beyond the beachhead. The landings in this area also positioned Allied divisions to protect the flank of the forces tasked with capturing Saint-Lô, Bayeux, and Caen. The U.S. Army's VII Corps—consisting of just over thirty thousand fighting men—received the critical mission of storming ashore near Les Dunes de Varreville and linking up with the two U.S. airborne divisions in the interior. At 6:30 a.m. on D-Day, the 8th Infantry Regiment, 4th Infantry Division spearheaded the amphibious assault landing but did so one mile south of the landing sector designated by the invasion plan. Despite this mislanding, the assistant division commander, Brig. Gen. Theodore Roosevelt, Jr., chose to push inland from the actual point of landing rather than attempt to move the assault force up the beach to the intended spot. Although this decision would ultimately introduce complications, the 4th Division proceeded inland against light opposition, swiftly linking up with the airborne troops who had landed before dawn. By the end of the day, both the 4th Infantry Division and the 358th and 359th Infantry Regiments of the 90th Infantry Division were ashore, intact, and engaged with enemy forces.

ABOVE: Troops from the U.S. Army's 4th Infantry Division wade ashore on Utah Beach on June 6. Five VLA antiaircraft barrage balloons have already been positioned on the beach to discourage a strafing attack. *U.S. Coast Guard Collection in the U.S. National Archives 26-G-2412* **RIGHT:** Another photograph taken inside the same LCVP just off of Utah Beach on D-Day. In addition to troops wading toward the shore, two DUKWs on the beach, and eight barrage balloons in the air, LCT-779 can be seen aground on the left. *U.S. Coast Guard Collection in the U.S. National Archives 26-G-2415*

OPPOSITE ABOVE: An aerial view of the landings on Utah Beach on D-Day showing three LCTs, an LCI, and four LCVPs as well as vehicles and personnel. **OPPOSITE BELOW:** Personnel from A Company, 261st Medical Battalion, 1st Engineer Special Brigade wading ashore on Utah Beach shortly after 10 a.m. on June 6, 1944. These men departed Plymouth Harbor at 7:30 a.m. on Monday, June 5, 1944, aboard LCI(L)-211, and, once they reached the Baie de la Seine, they transferred to the LCM seen here for the final run into the beach. Six surgical teams from the 3rd Auxiliary Surgical Group landed with the 261st Medical Battalion that day.

This photograph shows Brig. Gen. Theodore Roosevelt, Jr., son of President Theodore Roosevelt, in Sainte-Mère-Église shortly after D-Day. As the Assistant Division Commander of the 4th Infantry Division, he landed during the initial assault on Utah Beach on June 6. Showing a lack of concern for being under enemy fire, General Roosevelt rallied groups of men on the beach and personally led them across the seawall. In recognition of his "seasoned, precise, calm, and unfaltering leadership" at the very front of the attack that day, he was ultimately awarded the Medal of Honor. He never knew this, though, because he died from a coronary thrombosis during the night of July 12, 1944. *National Archives and Records Administration/US Army Signal Corps 111-SC-191911*

A Dodge WC52 3/4-ton Weapons Carrier moves through the surf toward the Tare Green sector of Utah Beach after driving off of its landing craft on June 6, 1944. Note that the vehicle is armed with an M2HB .50-caliber machine gun and is packed full of supplies. The house in the sand dunes to the right of the frame, known as Chalet Rouge, provided an easily recognizable landmark on shore. *National Archives and Records Administration/US Army Signal Corps 111-SC-190438*

Soldiers of the 8th Infantry Regiment, 4th Infantry Division escort German prisoners of war to an enclosure on Utah Beach. The 4th Division spearheaded the VII Corps landings on the Cotentin Peninsula on D-Day, and the 8th Infantry Regiment spearheaded the divisional assault. On the left, a Sherman tank from the 70th Tank Battalion cuts tracks in the sands of La Madeleine.

Navy Beach Battalion members dive for cover during a German strafing attack against VII Corps forces in the dunes at La Madeleine on Utah Beach. Note the concrete seawall on the left and the "hedgehog" beach obstacles that have been removed from the water and piled together on the beach. *U.S. Navy photograph, now in the collections of the US National Archives 80-G-252841*

German prisoners move into the barbed-wire enclosure set up to hold them on Utah Beach on D-Day. The soldier on the far left is eating from his *fettbüchse* (butter dish). Two LCTs can be seen on the beach in the background as well as five Rhino ferries and a fording-kit M5A1 Stewart Light Tank.

Utah Beach as seen from the tank deck of an LST. At the base of the ramp, two Jeeps have pulled up with casualties for evacuation as a column of German prisoners marches past. Note the U.S. Navy–marked M1 Heavy Tractor/International Harvester TD-18, the DUKW at the center right, and two GMC CCKW 2.5-ton cargo trucks on the beach. *U.S. Navy photograph, now in the collections of the US National Archives 80-G-252779*

An officer from either the 5th or 6th Engineer Special Brigade collects information from German prisoners on Utah Beach shortly after June 6. The soldier with the Asian features has been the subject of much speculation in the decades since this photograph was taken. The official caption identified the man as a "young Jap," but he was most certainly not of that extraction. In the 1990s, a theory emerged that he was a Korean impressed into the Japanese Imperial Army and then captured by the Russians before he was captured and conscripted into the service of the Third Reich. In recent years, he has even been identified as Yang Kyoungjong: a Korean conscript in the German Army who moved to the United States in 1947 and died in Illinois in April 1992. Since no evidence supporting this identity has been produced, the more convincing probability is that this soldier was a member of the 795th Georgian Battalion, a supporting unit in the German 709th Infantry Division composed of ethnically Georgian *osttruppen* (Eastern troops) positioned near Utah Beach at the time of the invasion. *U.S. Coast Guard Collection in the U.S. National Archives 26-G-2391*

Weighing in at just over three hundred thousand pounds, LCT-528 sits high and dry on Utah Beach while crewmen relax on her bow ramp waiting for the high tide to return. This landing craft was built by Bison Shipbuilding Corporation of North Tonawanda, New York, in 1943. *U.S. Navy photograph, now in the collections of the US National Archives 80-G-253009*

ABOVE: A French-made APX 47mm antitank gun looks out over Utah Beach shortly after D-Day. Designed by Atelier de Puteaux (thus, the "APX") and adopted by the French military as the "canon de 47mm semi-automatique modèle 1937," the German military captured a large number of these weapons in 1940 and thereafter used them under the designation 4.7cm Pak 181(f). This one was emplaced as part of the armament of Widerstandsnest 5 at La Madeleine and was captured by the 4th Infantry Division on June 6. In the background, bulldozers work on the beach while a CCKW 2.5-ton Cargo Truck drives ashore from a Rhino ferry and an LCM motors back out to the fleet. *National Archives and Records Administration/US Army Signal Corps 111-SC-190233* **OPPOSITE TOP LEFT:** A USAAF P-47D fighter (serial number 42-26136) from the 373rd Fighter Group lies in the sand on Utah Beach where it crash-landed during the first week of the invasion. Note that contact with the sand during the belly landing scrubbed off part of the national insignia on the right wing. *U.S. Navy photograph, now in the collections of the US National Archives 80-G-253420* **OPPOSITE TOP RIGHT:** An M4 Sherman medium tank nicknamed "Cannonball" from Company C, 70th Tank Battalion that became trapped in a shell crater while driving toward Utah Beach on D-Day. The tank's deep-wading trunks are clearly visible as well as the mounting brackets for the T40 Whiz-Bang Rocket Launcher on either side of the turret. *U.S. Navy photograph, now in the collections of the US National Archives 80-G-252802* **OPPOSITE BOTTOM:** With a DUKW in the background, a member of the U.S. Navy's 2nd Beach Battalion tinkers with a captured German Goliath tracked mine, or "beetle," on Utah Beach on June 11, 1944. The Goliath was a radio-controlled mini tank that let the user remain under cover while sending explosives into enemy lines to detonate them. *U.S. Navy photograph, now in the collections of the US National Archives 80-G-252752*

One of the two Type H667 casemates of the Stützpunkt 9 complex at Les Dunes d'Audouville two miles north of Utah Beach. Although undoubtedly a dangerous and effective weapon, the 8.8cm Panzerabwehrkanone 43/41 that can be seen in the top photograph did not fire on VII Corps forces on D-Day because it faced toward the north. Today, the gun is gone, and the settling of sand has caused the casemate to roll a bit toward the water's edge.

ABOVE: Medics from the 4th Infantry Division treat one of their own on Utah Beach on D-Day. The man was wounded in the right leg, which has been bandaged. The medic kneeling at the center still wears his M1926 Inflatable Lifebelt, and next to him in the sand is an example of the ultra-rare Navy Canvas Carrying Case (supply number 14-035). **RIGHT:** Sailors of the 2nd Naval Beach Battalion in the dunes at La Madeleine overlooking Utah Beach shortly after D-Day. A group of four DUKWs is behind them, and an LCT is approaching the beach beyond that. The same spot has changed little in seventy years. *U.S. Navy photograph, now in the collections of the US National Archives 80-G-252734.* **BELOW LEFT:** Men of the 1st Engineer Special Brigade dig in among the beach grass in front of Chalet Rouge at La Madeleine. Owned by the Lepelletier family in 1944, the house sits 1,613 feet (491 meters) north of the 4.7cm Panzerabwehrkanone 181(f) that was at the center of Widerstandsnest 5. **BELOW RIGHT:** This aerial photograph of the beach at La Madeleine shows the general area of Widerstandsnest 5 and, therefore, the spot where the U.S. Army's VII Corps made its assault landing on the morning of D-Day. The distinctive red-tile roof of the Chalet Rouge can be seen at the bottom right, and the road leading to Sainte-Marie-du-Mont (D913) can be seen running along the bottom of the horseracing track.

ABOVE LEFT: A soldier from the 90th Infantry Division speaks into the handset of his SCR-300 radio on Utah Beach. An M1936 Cartridge Belt leans against the radio, and the soldier's M1 Carbine has been laid in the grass next to him. He must have just come ashore because he still wears an M1926 Inflatable Lifebelt. **ABOVE RIGHT:** Three men from the 2nd Naval Beach Battalion, including a hospital corpsman, rest against the outside of one of the German shelters of Widerstandsnest 5 at La Madeleine. The bunker they are leaning against, which bears the scars of the fighting on D-Day, has been painted to look like an unthreatening house. The Germans had used the structure as a communications center, and the U.S. Army quickly put it to use as the same thing. Several dozen M1926 Inflatable Lifebelts are piled in front of the men, and a Dodge WC56 Command Car from the 915th Field Artillery Battalion, 90th Infantry Division gets directions from a military policeman in the background.

ABOVE LEFT: A German land mine is detonated by U.S. Army engineers of the 531st Engineer Shore Regiment just inland from Widerstandsnest 5 at Utah Beach. Two CCKW 2.5-ton Cargo Trucks have driven over the dunes on a path stabilized by SMT. The buildings of La Madeleine can be seen in the background. *U.S. Navy photograph, now in the collections of the US National Archives 80-G-252259* **ABOVE RIGHT:** Soldiers of the 4th Infantry Division advance inland across an area that has been swept for land mines and marked clear by the white strips of tape that can be seen going up and over the dunes in the background. The man at the far left is carrying the tripod for the M1917A1 .30-caliber water-cooled machine gun and four Mk II fragmentation hand grenades suspended around his neck by string. The man at the right is carrying an M1 Garand rifle still wrapped in a Pliofilm bag, and a medic behind him is carrying a stretcher and wearing an M7 Assault Gas Mask Bag. *National Archives and Records Administration/US Army Signal Corps 111-SC-190467*

LEFT: Two columns of soldiers from the 22nd Infantry Regiment, 4th Infantry Division are seen here crossing the flooded marsh behind Utah Beach on their way to Saint-Martin-de-Varreville on D-Day. Some still wear their M1926 Inflatable Lifebelts and M7 Assault Gas Mask Bags. The man at the far left is wearing an Assistant Gunner's Belt for the Browning Automatic Rifle, and he carries an M1 Garand rifle. Directly behind him, the gunner carries an M1918A2 Browning Automatic Rifle slung on his right shoulder. The man on the right is carrying an M1 rifle still wrapped in a Pliofilm bag over his shoulder, and the man behind him carries his Garand with a web rifle sling. **BELOW:** Soldiers of the 8th Infantry Regiment, 4th Infantry Division slosh across the flooded marshland behind Utah Beach after having just come ashore. The soldier closest to the camera offers an especially interesting case study of the specialized equipment carried by troops conducting the Operation Neptune amphibious landing. He carries an M7 Assault Gas Mask Bag strapped to his chest and an M1 Garand rifle enclosed in a Pliofilm bag. Since the bag prevented use of the rifle's sling, this man carries his rifle with a length of rope instead. He also carries an M1 Bazooka Antitank Rocket Launcher with an inflated M1926 Lifebelt attached to avoid losing it while wading ashore. *National Archives and Records Administration/ US Army Signal Corps 111-SC-190061*

RIGHT: A disabled Duplex Drive M4 Sherman tank from the 70th Tank Battalion sits off to the side of one of the causeways leading inland from Utah Beach. These raised macadam roadways, often referred to as beach exits, provided the invasion force's heavy vehicles their only means of circulating from the beachhead at La Madeleine into the interior. Recognizing the critical importance of these beach exits, German fighting forces covered them with registered artillery fire and antitank guns. This Duplex Drive Sherman was one of the first to push inland from the beach and was also among the first to fall victim to an antitank gun. **BELOW:** After having landed at Utah Beach, men of the 12th Infantry Regiment, 4th Infantry Division move into the interior using Beach Exit 3 leading to the village of Audoville-la-Hubert. The area off to either side of the roadway shows signs of the deliberate flooding employed to restrict movement of a landing force. The knocked-out Duplex Drive Sherman seen in the previous photograph is behind the second man, but a fresh 70th Tank Battalion Sherman is coming up behind it. Having tank support for the infantry in the initial assault phase was critical to establishment of the beachhead.

ABOVE: As the assault force landed, it spread out like octopus tentacles to follow the three lower beach exits. The 4th Infantry Division led the way, but it was followed by elements of the 90th Infantry Division. Here, men of the 90th Division's 357th Infantry Regiment pause along Beach Exit 1 leading to Pouppeville during the afternoon of June 8. A sign along the hedgerow on the right side of the roadway indicates that mines are in the area, which is probably why the advance has come to a halt. These men are clearly part of a heavy-weapons company because some of the equipment associated with that kind of unit can be seen here: the tripod for an M1917A1 Water-cooled Heavy Machine Gun, cans of belted .30-caliber ammunition, and the M2 Ammunition Carrying Vest. An officer from the 1st Engineer Special Brigade is walking toward the front of the column. *National Archives and Records Administration/US Army Signal Corps 111-SC-320892* **LEFT:** A soldier from the 1st Battalion, 8th Infantry Regiment carrying an M1917A1 Heavy Machine Gun and a belt of .30-caliber ammunition passes through La Madeleine after landing on Utah Beach. The house behind him served as the command post for Oberleutnant Matz, the German officer from 3, Grenadier Regiment 919, who commanded Widerstandsnest 5. This machine gunner still wears his lifebelt and assault gas mask bag. Attached to his M1936 Pistol Belt is an M1911A1 .45-caliber Pistol in its holster and an M1910 entrenching tool. *National Archives and Records Administration/US Army Signal Corps 111-SC-190466*

5

POINTE du HOC

A FORCE OF 225 MEN from the U.S. Army's 2nd Ranger Battalion received the special D-Day mission of landing at the base of Pointe du Hoc four miles west of Omaha Beach and scaling the cliffs there to conduct an assault against one of the most threatening German gun batteries in lower Normandy. Established in May 1942, Heeres-Küsten-Batterie Pointe du Hoc (WN75) was a position armed with six French-made 155mm breech-loading rifles. These guns had been captured in 1940 and subsequently placed in German Army service with the designation 15.5cm K 418(f). At Pointe du Hoc, they were mounted on concrete traversing tables that extended their maximum effective range, tightened their already impressive accuracy, and transformed them into formidable

LEFT: One of the few photographs capturing Rangers in combat at Pointe du Hoc. Probably taken on June 7, the image shows an NCO (top right) firing an M1919A4 .30-caliber Machine Gun from a fighting position at the cliff's edge. By his right foot are six cans of belted ammunition, providing an additional 1,500 rounds of .30-caliber cartridges for the weapon. On his M1936 Pistol Belt are an M1910 Entrenching Tool and an M17 Leather Field Glasses Case. The Ranger to his left wears the canvas assault vest with an M1910 Entrenching Tool attached to it. The Ranger at the far left has an M3 Trench Knife in an M8 Scabbard attached to his M1936 Cartridge Belt. A Ranger officer has his back to the camera at the bottom right. *National Archives and Records Administration 111-SC-320894*

RIGHT: A formation of Douglas A-20 Havoc light bombers flies northward to return to its base in England after just having bombed Heeres-Küsten-Batterie Pointe du Hoc (Army Coast Artillery Battery Pointe du Hoc). The repeated bombing of the site extensively damaged the concrete tables upon which the guns were mounted, ultimately resulting in their removal about five weeks before the invasion. *U.S. National Archives and Records Administration*

ABOVE: In this June 2010 aerial photograph of Pointe du Hoc, the heavy cratering caused by bombing and shelling during World War II can be seen clearly. At that time, a French engineering firm was working to stabilize the cliff face and the Type R636a battery command/fire control post bunker, which is why pieces of construction equipment are present on the site. This preservation project was done in cooperation with Texas A&M University's Center for Heritage Conservation.

anti-ship weapons. The Ranger mission on D-Day, which was commanded by Lt. Col. James Earl Rudder, had the objective of preventing these guns from firing on the fleet.

At 7:10 a.m., Rudder's force landed from nine British Landing Craft, Assault (LCA), scaled the cliffs, and swiftly pushed the enemy back from the battery area. That is when the Rangers discovered that no guns were mounted at the point. Instead, timbers had been placed on each of the six concrete traversing tables to make it look as if the battery remained armed. The Rangers also found two casemates for heavy artillery at Pointe du Hoc (of Type H679), but they were still under construction, and their guns had not yet been mounted. In late April, the Germans had removed the guns from the point to a position almost a mile to the south in the hedgerows near La Montagne, but the Rangers did not know that. After they secured the WN75 battery position, they moved on to the next phase of their mission, which was to set up a roadblock on the Vierville/Grandcamp road (present-day D514). While doing this, the Rangers put out flank security and quickly stumbled across the guns concealed along a hedgerow-enclosed lane. First Sergeant Leonard "Bud" Lomell and Staff Sgt. Jack Kuhn then disabled the guns using Thermite grenades. Overnight on June 6 and 7, the Germans launched a series of powerful counterattacks from the direction of Grandcamp-Maisy, which pushed the Rangers back to the point. By the time vehicles from Omaha Beach linked up with Rudder's force at Pointe du Hoc on June 7, the Rangers had suffered 135 casualties, most of which happened during the German counterattacks on the night of June 6.

A view of Pointe du Hoc taken from the west looking toward Îles Saint-Marcouf and the east coast of the Cotentin Peninsula. Utah Beach can be seen in the background just above the memorial on the battery command/fire control post.

ABOVE: Looking down on the point from the R636a fire control post bunker. The barbed wire that can be found around the site today was not there during the war. **BELOW:** A view from the gravel beach on the east side of Pointe du Hoc at low tide. *Courtesy of Paul Woodadge*

TOP: A Canon de 155mm modele 1917 in transit configuration but abandoned along the side of the road somewhere in France in 1940. Designed by Col. Louis Jean François Filloux, this weapon was referred to as *grande puissance Filloux*, or simply "GPF" for short. The Germans captured more than four hundred GPFs with the fall of France and, recognizing their outstanding quality, used them throughout the war under the designation 15.5cm K 418(f). Heeres-Küsten-Batterie Pointe du Hoc was armed with six GPFs. **ABOVE:** The six 15.5cm K 418(f)s that armed Heeres-Küsten-Batterie Pointe du Hoc were mounted on open concrete traversing tables that extended their range and enhanced their accuracy. Although the gun was a piece of field artillery, this mounting system transformed the GPF into a dangerous and powerful coast artillery weapon. **RIGHT:** One of the six GPFs that armed Heeres-Küsten-Batterie Pointe du Hoc remains at the site today, although its carriage is gone. **BELOW LEFT:** This marking above the breech on the GPF at Pointe du Hoc today indicates that Atelier de Puteaux in Paris manufactured it in 1917. **BELOW RIGHT:** The lower breech marking on the GPF at Pointe du Hoc today reveals serial number 20.

ABOVE: A view of the eastern side of Pointe du Hoc from the beach showing the spoil pile created when 14-inch shells from the battleship USS *Texas* (BB-35) struck the face of the cliff. *Official U.S. Navy photograph, now in the collections of the National Archives 80-G-45718*

RIGHT: Because each of the six GPFs at Pointe du Hoc weighed over twenty-eight thousand pounds, each sat on a steel tray equipped with twelve rollers that rode on a concrete pintle block. This system evenly distributed the weapon's weight and permitted 360 degrees of traverse. Although it is often overlooked, one of the steel trays remains on the site today.

This may be the area where the Rangers who landed from LCA-888 managed to climb to the top using an extension ladder placed on a mound of debris knocked out of the cliff top. Although this photo was taken on D+2 (June 8, 1944) when the route was being used for supplies, it nevertheless illustrates the great difficulty associated with getting up the cliffs in the initial assault. A toggle rope and two plain ropes can be seen below the ladder. *Official U.S. Navy photograph, now in the collections of the National Archives 80-G-45716*

After the German soldiers of 2, Heeres-Küsten-Artillerie-Regiment, 1260 (the 2nd Battalion, Army Coast Artillery Regiment 1260) removed the GPFs from Pointe du Hoc during the night of April 25–26, 1944, they replaced them with timbers and wooden beams, hoping they would give the impression that the battery remained armed. Here, Sgt. Warden F. Lowell inspects one of the dummy pieces on June 8, 1944.

OPPOSITE: In this 1975 aerial photograph of the area around Saint-Pierre-du-Mont, Le Guay, La Montagne, and Pointe du Hoc, the six small yellow circles indicate the location of the six concrete traversing tables for the GPFs/15.5cm K 418(f)s, and the elongated yellow circle at the bottom left indicates the position of the guns on D-Day.

LEFT: When five of the Pointe du Hoc GPFs were relocated five weeks before the invasion, they were moved up this dirt road at La Montagne.

BELOW: This photograph was taken facing toward the west from the spot where five of the six GPFs from Pointe du Hoc were found on D-Day. In the distance just to the left of the buildings across the field, you can clearly see the Utah Beach landing area at La Madeleine 8.5 miles away.

ABOVE LEFT: One of the Pointe du Hoc GPFs is seen here in its hedgerow position near La Montagne. Without the stabilized concrete mount built for it at the point, the weapon would not have been quite as accurate, and its range would have been slightly reduced. Nevertheless, this GPF would have easily been capable of delivering accurate fire missions against targets landing on Utah Beach at La Madeleine. **ABOVE RIGHT:** In this photograph, taken shortly after D-Day, another of the Pointe du Hoc GPFs can be seen with its muzzle pointing over a cattle gate. Although the guns' fire would have been slightly less dangerous from the position near La Montagne, the hedgerows concealed the GPFs from the Allied air attacks that were increasing in regularity during the weeks that preceded the invasion. **BELOW:** Two U.S. Army Rangers pose on the right split trail of the GPF seen in the photograph above. The wooden planks on the ground between the trails span a pit that has been excavated beneath the weapon's breech to allow room for the gun tube to move through full recoil when firing at high elevation. Note that the weapon's sight and breechblock are still in place.

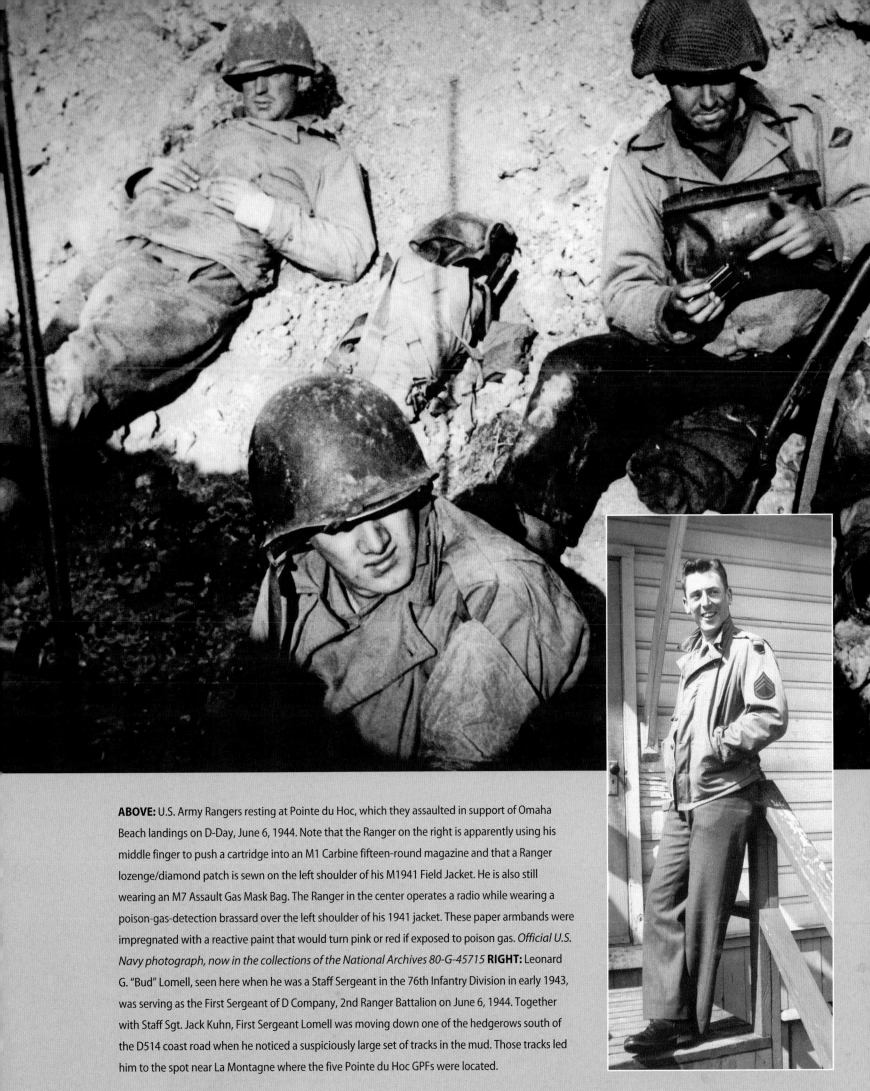

ABOVE: U.S. Army Rangers resting at Pointe du Hoc, which they assaulted in support of Omaha Beach landings on D-Day, June 6, 1944. Note that the Ranger on the right is apparently using his middle finger to push a cartridge into an M1 Carbine fifteen-round magazine and that a Ranger lozenge/diamond patch is sewn on the left shoulder of his M1941 Field Jacket. He is also still wearing an M7 Assault Gas Mask Bag. The Ranger in the center operates a radio while wearing a poison-gas-detection brassard over the left shoulder of his 1941 jacket. These paper armbands were impregnated with a reactive paint that would turn pink or red if exposed to poison gas. *Official U.S. Navy photograph, now in the collections of the National Archives 80-G-45715* **RIGHT:** Leonard G. "Bud" Lomell, seen here when he was a Staff Sergeant in the 76th Infantry Division in early 1943, was serving as the First Sergeant of D Company, 2nd Ranger Battalion on June 6, 1944. Together with Staff Sgt. Jack Kuhn, First Sergeant Lomell was moving down one of the hedgerows south of the D514 coast road when he noticed a suspiciously large set of tracks in the mud. Those tracks led him to the spot near La Montagne where the five Pointe du Hoc GPFs were located.

ABOVE: This photograph of Lt. Col. James Earl Rudder's command post at Pointe du Hoc's eastern Type L409A antiaircraft bunker was taken in the afternoon on D-Day and reveals the many purposes a command post had to serve in combat: communications center, medical aid station, casualty collecting point, supply depot, etc. Perhaps the most intriguing thing about this photograph is the assortment of known individuals shown in it. The man with his head bandaged at the bottom right is Lt. Col. Tom Trevor, a British commando who accompanied the Ranger assault force as an observer. The man to the left of the radio antennae loading a magazine for his M1 Carbine is Lt. Elmer H. "Dutch" Vermeer, 2nd Ranger Battalion Engineer Officer. *Official U.S. Navy photograph, now in the collections of the National Archives 80-G-45721* **RIGHT:** Another photograph showing Lieutenant Colonel Rudder's command post at Pointe du Hoc's eastern Type L409A antiaircraft bunker. Note the forty-eight-star U.S. flag being used to identify the position to ships offshore and aircraft overhead. German prisoners are being marched away under armed guard just above and to the left of the flag. *National Archives and Records Administration 111-SC-190240*

ABOVE: With a load of walking wounded Rangers from the Pointe du Hoc battle embarked aboard, LCM-81 pulls alongside a transport during the afternoon of June 6, 1944. For the first few days of the invasion, landing craft represented the only way to get supplies into and the wounded off of the point. *Official U.S. Navy photograph, now in the collections of the National Archives 26-G-2368* **LEFT:** Here, two Rangers have captured three German soldiers along with three Italian and four French laborers from Organisation Todt, the Third Reich workforce responsible for civil and military engineering projects. The laborers were at Pointe du Hoc to complete the two Type H679 casemates still under construction at the time of the invasion. LCVPs took twenty-seven prisoners off of the point on the afternoon of June 7, including the ten men seen here. *National Archives and Records Administration 111-SC-190268*

RIGHT: One of the French laborers captured at Pointe du Hoc is searched after being brought aboard the battleship USS *Texas* (BB-35) on the evening of June 7. He is being guarded by a member of the ship's Marine detachment armed with a .45-caliber Reising Model 50 Submachine Gun. Although none of them went ashore on June 6, hundreds of U.S. Marines participated in the Normandy invasion. **BELOW:** Another scene on the deck of the *Texas* shows prisoners from Pointe du Hoc being brought aboard on D-Day. With dozens of the ship's crew looking on, an Italian laborer comes forward under the watchful eye of a Marine armed with a .45-caliber Reising Model 55 Submachine Gun. The prisoners only remained on *Texas* briefly before being transferred to an LST.

ABOVE LEFT: The battery command and fire control/observation post (a Type R636a bunker) at Stützpunkt Pointe du Hoc (WN75) after the battle. A textured facade has been built around the structure in an effort to camouflage it. *National Archives and Records Administration 111-SC-275839* **ABOVE RIGHT:** One of the Type H679 casemates under construction at Stützpunkt Pointe du Hoc (WN75) when the Rangers landed on D-Day. *National Archives and Records Administration 111-SC-275822* **BELOW LEFT:** Both of the Type H679 casemates at Stützpunkt Pointe du Hoc (WN75) suffered heavy damage during the fighting on D-Day and the days that immediately followed. *National Archives and Records Administration* **BELOW RIGHT:** One of the two Type L409A bunkers at Stützpunkt Pointe du Hoc (WN75). This position at one time mounted a 2cm Flugabwehrkanone 30 antiaircraft gun, but the weapon was removed because of the damage to the concrete. *National Archives and Records Administration 111-SC-275825*

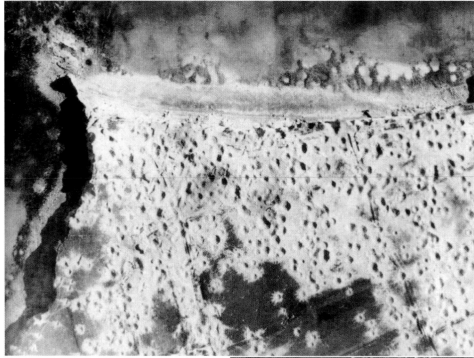

ABOVE: In this June 10, 1944, aerial photograph of Pointe du Hoc, the heavy cratering from bombing and shelling is clearly in evidence. **RIGHT:** A U.S. Army officer stands inside one of the craters at Stützpunkt Pointe du Hoc (WN75) after the battle. The width and depth of the crater clearly indicates the earthmoving power of the bomb that caused it.
National Archives and Records Administration 111-SC-275840

This memorial to a fallen soldier stands amid the craters and debris of battle at Stützpunkt Pointe du Hoc (WN75). Here a U.S. M1 Helmet has been placed on top of the handgrip of a Vickers K Gun, the muzzle of which is stuck in the soil. Although they were British weapons chambered for the .303-caliber cartridge, K Guns were used during the battle at Pointe du Hoc mounted on the ends of extending ladders that were, in turn, mounted on DUKWs. A belt of German 7.92x57mm cartridges lies on a wooden crate in the foreground, and a spent U.S. M22 Colored Smoke Rifle Grenade is just above it. The K Gun's drum magazine is in the dirt at the far right. *Official U.S. Navy photograph, now in the collections of the National Archives 26-G-2441*

Just a few days after D-Day, the 9th Tactical Air Command Signal Section set up camp in the orchard near La Montagne. During their time there, the men of this unit got a close-up look at the 155mm guns from Pointe du Hoc and sometimes even posed for photographs on them. Here, Pvt. Roy Vanderpolder and Pvt. Orville Iverson are sitting on one of the GPFs, which has been pulled from its firing position and deactivated by removal of its breechblock.

On Monday, June 12, 1944, a number of high-ranking U.S. military leaders visited the orchard at La Montagne to see the GPFs that had once armed Stützpunkt Pointe du Hoc (WN75). The officers in this photograph are Lt. Gen. Henry A. "Hap" Arnold, General Eisenhower, Adm. Alan G. Kirk, and (with his back to the camera) U.S. Army Chief of Staff General George C. Marshall. Note that the weapon's breech is open and that wooden planks have been laid across the recoil pit beneath it.

ABOVE: As soon as the corridor between Omaha Beach and Pointe du Hoc was secure, the 834th Engineer Aviation Battalion began building this temporary airfield parallel to D514 just east of Saint-Pierre-du-Mont. At first just an Emergency Landing Strip, then a Refueling and Rearming Strip, it ultimately became Advanced Landing Ground A-1 with a single five-thousand-foot SMT runway. Fighters, bombers, and transport aircraft made extensive use of A-1 before it was ultimately dismantled in September 1944. In this photograph of the airfield, Pointe du Hoc can be seen in the upper left corner, and P-38 Lightning fighters are parked in the field next to Ferme de Valmont, the cluster of buildings at the bottom left.

BELOW: Lomell ultimately received the Distinguished Service Cross for finding and disabling the Pointe du Hoc GPFs on D-Day, and he was eventually promoted to the rank of second lieutenant. Seen here at the end of the war, this citizen soldier finished his time in the Army a highly decorated Ranger and uniquely experienced combat leader. Lomell received his honorable discharge in December 1945, went

to law school, and was admitted to the New Jersey Bar in 1951.

RIGHT ABOVE: Lomell went back to Pointe du Hoc for the first time in 1964 with his wife, Charlotte, which is when he posed for this photograph in front of one of the site's Type H679 casemates.

RIGHT BELOW: The same casemate has not changed much in seventy years.

ABOVE: Lomell also posed on the stairs leading down into the troop shelter/ready ammunition storage area for one of the concrete traversing tables on the eastern side of Pointe du Hoc. In the foreground, the tip of the table's pintle rod can be seen, and in the background is one of the site's Type H679 casemates. **BELOW:** During his first return trip in 1964, Lomell paused to contemplate the spot where he scaled the cliffs at Pointe du Hoc twenty years earlier. With a long list of awards and accolades that ultimately brought him to the attention of celebrities, renowned journalists, and presidents, it is obvious that Lomell's greatness was only getting started when he landed on this beach on D-Day. He passed away on March 1, 2011, of natural causes in Toms River, New Jersey.

ABOVE: Pointe du Hoc was chosen as the spot where Ronald Wilson Reagan, the fortieth president of the United States, would deliver his main address during the commemorative activities surrounding the fortieth anniversary of D-Day. From a podium on top of the Type R636a battery command/fire control post bunker, he set a bold, new tone for the U.S. memorialization of World War II with these words: "These are the boys of Pointe du Hoc. These are the men who took the cliffs. These are the champions who helped free a continent. These are the heroes who helped end a war." **OPPOSITE ABOVE:** President Reagan and First Lady Nancy Reagan inside the telemetry room of the Type R636a battery command/fire control post bunker at Pointe du Hoc during their visit on the morning of June 6, 1984. **OPPOSITE BELOW:** The Ranger Memorial on top of the Type R636a bunker at Pointe du Hoc looks out over an uncharacteristically calm Baie de la Seine on July 24, 2011.

6

LA FIÈRE

MANOIR DE LA FIÈRE is a small settlement of stone buildings just west of Sainte-Mère-Église that in June 1944 was owned by Monsieur Louis Leroux. Because of its strategic location astride the Merderet River, the manor was one of the primary D-Day objectives of Maj. Gen. Matthew B. Ridgway's 82nd Airborne Division. Normally little more than a narrow, meandering creek, the Merderet's condition was far from normal in June 1944. It had transformed into a huge, shallow lake 3/5 of a mile wide by 6 1/4 miles long. The virtually impassable inundated area produced by the flood-stage river separated the Amfreville/Motey area to the west from the city of Carentan and the villages of Chef-du-Pont and Sainte-Mère-Église to the east.

LEFT: La Fière Manor and the D15 bridge over the Merderet River as seen from the air in June 2010. This small cluster of seven buildings became the scene of a vicious battle just after dawn on D-Day.

ABOVE: This aerial view of the area surrounding the La Fière causeway shows the following: 1. La Fière Manor, 2. the Merderet River Bridge at La Fière, 3. La Fière causeway, 4. the chapel at Cauqigny, 5. Hameau aux Brix, and 6. Les Heutes/Timmes' Orchard. **RIGHT:** Seen here in 1946, La Fière Manor still shows signs of the damage it sustained during the fighting in June 1944. The roof of the southern half of the main house is almost completely missing. Note that the Sainte-Mère-Église/Amfreville road (now D15) was not paved back then.

The U.S. invasion plan called for the establishment and then the expansion of a beachhead at La Madeleine on the east coast of the Cotentin Peninsula, followed by a drive north toward Cherbourg. For the U.S. Army VII Corps—the force tasked with establishing that beachhead—the swollen condition of the Merderet River would present a difficult obstacle. With infantry and mechanized units pouring across Utah Beach, the road networks leading into the interior of the Cotentin and across the Merderet would be strategically crucial.

The 82nd Airborne's three parachute infantry regiments had each been given mission objectives in the Sainte-Mère-Église area during this operation. According to this plan, the 508th Parachute Infantry would capture the Douve River crossings to the southwest. The 505th Parachute Infantry would take Sainte-Mère-Église itself, as well as the eastern ends of the Merderet River crossings at Chef-du-Pont and La Fière. By dropping near Amfreville, the 507th Parachute Infantry would be in a position to capture the western end of the La Fière causeway: the tiny village of Cauquigny. There, an elevated roadway stretched five hundred yards across the inundated Merderet basin to La Fière on the east bank. Holding Cauquigny, La

Manoir de la Fière suffered extensive damage during the fighting that took place around it between June 6 and 9. This photograph provides evidence of the pounding the manor's main house received.

Fière, and the causeway stretching between them would give the U.S. Army VII Corps back at the beach the open artery over the swollen river it needed. Failure to secure the Merderet River crossings could spell disaster for VII Corps. Taking Sainte-Mère-Église, Chef-du-Pont, and the bridge and causeway at La Fière during the first hours of the invasion was of the utmost importance.

Inconveniently, twenty-eight German infantrymen arrived at Manoir de la Fière at 11 p.m. on Monday, June 5, to establish an outpost. Roused out of bed, Monsieur Leroux and his family were surprised by their arrival because, strangely, no German soldiers had ever occupied the manor before. Thus, as the men of the 82nd Airborne were being flown across the English Channel during the predawn hours of D-Day, the German soldiers they would soon face at La Fière were just beginning to settle in and prepare their defenses, setting the stage for battle.

The mission that dropped the 82nd Airborne Division on June 6, 1944, was codenamed "Boston," and it did not go perfectly according to plan in the skies above the Cotentin. As the 378 C-47s carrying the division's three parachute infantry regiments approached their drop zones, they encountered thick cloud cover and German antiaircraft fire. The combination of low visibility and flak produced a scattered drop. Out of the three regiments, the 505th was the luckiest, with most of its sticks coming down between Sainte-Mère-Église and the Merderet. The 508th and 507th did not experience similar fortune. Many of the 508th sticks ended up west of the river in the vicinity of Picauville and Pont-l'Abbé, while a large number of 507th sticks were dropped east of their drop zone in the inundated area of the Merderet River. Most of the paratroopers who landed

ABOVE LEFT: The central yard of La Fière Manor as seen from the second floor of the main house. Outbuildings in this photograph include the stable, barn, and mill. The Merderet River Bridge, which is mostly obscured by bushes to the left of the white gate, is at the center; beyond that, the causeway can be seen as it bends toward the northwest. The stone building in the distance at the center is the chapel at Cauquigny 2,053 feet (625 meters) away.
ABOVE RIGHT: The Merderet River Bridge at La Fière as it appeared in July 1944 when army historian S.L.A. Marshall visited the site shortly after the battle. Note the rough condition of the road surfacing and the concrete telephone pole. The distance from the main house at La Fière Manor to the bridge is barely one hundred feet. **OPPOSITE:** This Marshall photograph, taken from the middle of the Merderet River Bridge at La Fière, looks west toward Cauquigny. Compared to the way the same spot looks today, there was much more foliage present along the causeway in 1944.

there were driven by instinct toward the dry ground closest to them, which just so happened to be the Carentan/Cherbourg railroad embankment. Once there, they followed the embankment south to its junction with the road to Sainte-Mère-Église (present-day D15), and from there, La Fière Manor sat only eight hundred yards to the west along good road. Since La Fière Manor was one of the division's main objectives, several groups of the 82nd Airborne's paratroopers began moving toward it during the predawn hours of D-Day.

The opening shots of the battle for La Fière were fired at dawn when an MG42 in the manor's main house opened on troopers of Lt. John J. "Red Dog" Dolan's A Company, 505th Parachute Infantry. The twenty-eight German soldiers who had arrived to occupy the manor the night before were not going to give up without a fight. Dolan's 505th troopers then attempted to flank the enemy by maneuvering around to attack the right (or north) side of the manor. In so doing, they ran into more small-arms and machine-gun fire. A force of eighty 507th paratroopers being led by G Company Commander Capt. "Ben" Schwartzwalder then joined the battle. What was developing at La Fière Manor that morning was a fight in which several units simultaneously converged on the same objective in a piecemeal, uncoordinated manner. Captain Schwartzwalder had his men cross the road and enter the fields on its south side. Once in the fields, they began moving cautiously toward their objective.

La Fière Manor was surrounded by mainly pasture on its western side, with orchards and earthen mounds to the east. A vast network of crisscrossing hedgerows dominated its eastern approaches from the direction of Sainte-Mère-Église—the area through which the 82nd would have to fight. After moving only a short distance, Schwartzwalder's group came under fire from a German machine gun in the manor—one of the same

ABOVE: A mere 75 feet in length, the old stone bridge at La Fière became critically important at the outset of the invasion because it, along with the 1,500-foot-long causeway leading beyond it to Cauquigny, offered one of only two crossing points of the flooded Merderet River.

OPPOSITE: Looking northeast from the middle of La Fière bridge, these photographs show that very little has changed since Marshall took the top photograph seventy years ago. In the modern photograph, the church at Neuville-au-Plain can be seen 2.5 miles in the distance, but it is obscured by dense foliage in the 1944 photograph.

machine guns that had stopped Dolan's 505th paratroopers earlier in the morning. At about that same time, 508th regimental commander Col. Roy Lindquist arrived on the scene with a group of troopers that included men from C Company, 505th. With a minimum of coordination, these units continued to converge until elements of the 505th and the 508th began to enter the manor grounds through the backyard. Sporadic return fire continued briefly until one of the A Company, 505th men advancing with Dolan pulled the trigger on his MIAI Bazooka rocket launcher and a 2.36-inch rocket slammed into the stoutly built stone house. Then a 508th sergeant by the name of Palmer darted through the front door and emptied a full magazine from his Thompson submachine gun up through the floorboards of the second story. What was left of the German force surrendered at that point, and the battle for the Leroux manor at La Fière was over.

Meanwhile, on the other end of the causeway, Lt. Col. Charles J. Timmes, commanding the 2nd Battalion of the 507th, was in an difficult position. He had landed on the correct side of the river with a group of men, but he could not establish communications with either his regiment or his division. Rather than move his force over to the east bank of the Merderet, Timmes placed his men in defensive positions at an apple orchard northeast of Le Motey at Les Heutes. He knew that he needed to occupy the western end of the La Fière causeway, so he ordered Lt. Louis Levy to take ten men and outpost the village of Cauquigny. When Levy's patrol arrived there around noon, they found Cauquigny clear of the enemy.

ABOVE: Tanks of Panzer Ersatz und Ausbildungs Abteilung 100 (100th Tank Replacement and Training Battalion) knocked out during the intense fighting that unfolded on the La Fière causeway. All three of the vehicles seen here are French-made tanks that were captured in 1940: at the far left and far right are examples of the Renault R35, which was designated Panzerkampfwagen 35R 731(f) in German service. The tank in the center is a Hotchkiss H38/39, known as Panzerkampfwagen 38H 735(f) to the Germans. The section of track in the foreground belongs to the only German-made Panzerkampfwagen III Sonderkraftfahrzeug 141 in the battalion's inventory. This image was taken from a reel of motion-picture footage filmed by Signal Corps photographer T-4 Reuben A. Weiner of the 165th Signal Photo Company on June 10, 1944. **OPPOSITE:** This image from the Marshall series shows the bend in the La Fière causeway where so much intense combat unfolded on June 6 and 7 as elements of Panzer Ersatz und Ausbildungs Abteilung 100 and Grenadier Regiment 1057 attempted to recapture the La Fière causeway. The concrete telephone poles are gone now, and the foliage is not as thick, but the site remains easily recognizable nevertheless.

La Fière, Cauquigny, and the roadway stretching between them now belonged to the 82nd Airborne Division. Captain Schwartzwalder felt that the time was right for his force to cross over to the west bank and join the force at Timmes Orchard. When the company reached the west bank, Schwartzwalder left Lieutenant Levy and eight men to guard Cauquigny and then moved out in search of Lieutenant Colonel Timmes. At La Fière, paratroopers of the 505th dug in and prepared to defend the manor. Two bazooka teams positioned themselves near the bridge and dragged a disabled German truck into the middle of the causeway to act as a roadblock. Finally, the paratroopers positioned a 57mm antitank gun directly at the bend in the road above the manor, over-looking the causeway.

Aware of what was at stake at the La Fière crossing of the Merderet area, the Germans had already dispatched forces on the west bank to counterattack toward Cauquigny and the American bridgehead beyond. Soon, elements of the German 91 Luftland Division appeared west of Cauquigny, bearing down on the causeway. This force consisted of a rifle company from Grenadier Regiment 1057 and elements of Panzer Ersatz und Ausbildungs Abteilung 100 (100th Tank Training and Replacement Battalion), an armored training battalion equipped with mostly French-made Renault and Hotchkiss light tanks. With a Panzerkampfwagen III Sd.Kfz. 141 leading the column, the tanks and infantry quickly rolled over Lieutenant Levy's lightly armed force guarding Cauquigny in a skirmish that lasted only ten minutes. At that point, the Germans pushed onward across the causeway.

At approximately 5 p.m., the full weight of the armored counterattack fell on the para-troopers of Lieutenant Dolan's A Company, 505th in their positions around the bridge at

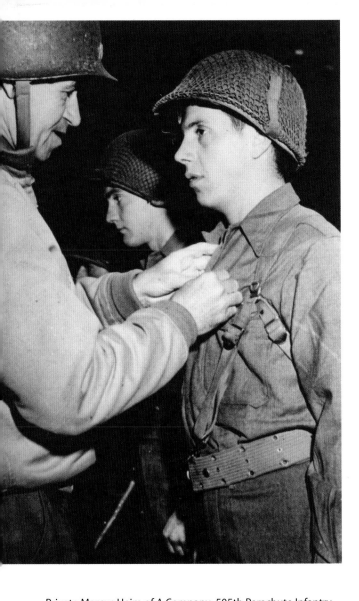

Although this photograph was taken on August 7, 1944, it shows a dump where U.S. forces collected some of the captured French tanks used by the Germans in Normandy. Recognizable here are four Renault R35s, eight Hotchkiss H39s, and an old Renault FT (the tenth tank from the left with the domed commander's cupola). These vehicles are from Panzer Ersatz und Ausbildungs Abteilung 100 and Panzer Abteilung 206, another tank unit based on the Cotentin Peninsula. The eighth vehicle—which can easily be picked out of the lineup by its distinctive long gun barrel equipped with a muzzle brake—is a Marder III Ausführung H, Sonderkraftfahrzeug 138, a tank destroyer produced by mounting the 7.5cm Panzerabwehrkanone 40 on the chassis of the pre-war Czech-designed Panzerkampfwagen 38(t). In all likelihood, the Marder was assigned to SS Panzerjäger Abteilung 17 of the 17 SS Panzer Grenadier Division.

Private Marcus Heim of A Company, 505th Parachute Infantry Regiment, 82nd Airborne Division receives the Distinguished Service Cross from Lt. Gen. Omar N. Bradley in La Haye-du-Puis on July 1, 1944. When the tanks attacked La Fière on D-Day, Private Heim was an assistant gunner with one of the bazooka teams defending the Merderet River Bridge. Since their fighting position was below the road behind a telephone pole, the two men were forced to stand when firing. Even when the tanks approached to within thirty yards, Heim remained with his gunner, Pfc. Lenold C. Peterson, reloading the rocket launcher as rapidly as possible. At first, branches obscured their field of fire, so the two paratroopers moved forward to continue fighting. In the middle of the battle, they ran out of rockets, forcing Private Heim to run from one side of the causeway to the other under fire to retrieve more from another position. Together, they put rockets into all three of the tanks, thereby helping to repulse the attack. For this, both men were awarded the Distinguished Service Cross. Today, the causeway is named Voie Marcus Heim in his honor.

These soldiers of the 325th Glider Infantry Regiment, 82nd Airborne Division have set up a position for an M1919A4 Machine Gun at the base of a typical Norman hedgerow. Throughout the Normandy campaign, both sides used the mounds upon which hedgerows grew as defensive positions. There are eight cans of belted .30-caliber ammunition in this photograph, equaling a total of two thousand rounds for the M1919A4. The man with his back to the camera is wearing an unusual ensemble: an M1941 Field Jacket, M1942 jump trousers, and rough-out service shoes with leggings—a mix of paratrooper and regular infantry uniform items.

La Fière. In the savage fight that followed, the Americans employed an M1A1 Bazooka and the lone 57mm antitank rifle to knock out the Panzerkampfwagen III and two French tanks. Then, concentrated fire from the paratroopers' M1 rifles and especially their .30-caliber machine guns tore viciously into the infantry exposed on the open road. Soon, the energy of the assault had been drained, and the Germans withdrew, having sustained heavy casualties.

The next morning (D+1), the Germans threw another combined assault at the paratroopers defending La Fière Manor. This time, the thrust was preceded by heavy supporting fire from mortars and artillery that had been brought in overnight. Just as the day before, the attack advanced as far as the outermost American defensive positions before grinding to a halt. The lone 57mm antitank gun knocked out the lead tank, after which German infantrymen swarmed forward. At point-blank range, the enemy tossed grenades and poured a relentless fire into the paratroopers using Mauser rifles and MP40 submachine guns. The men of Dolan's A Company, 505th at the foot of the bridge faced the full

In addition to the big guns of the 345th Field Artillery Battalion, the 82nd Airborne Division's mortars also contributed to the preparatory bombardment on Cauquigny on June 9. In this photo, an M1 81mm mortar team from the 325th Glider Infantry Regiment fires from a pit dug in the hedgerows near La Fière.

weight of the German assault, and the combat grew ferocious. But then the brutal attack mysteriously ended. The German infantry that had advanced almost to the bridge melted back toward Cauquigny in a fighting withdrawal. Although the paratroopers had survived another German onslaught, the situation at the causeway remained a stalemate, and the great, decisive battle was yet to be waged.

The 82nd Airborne soldiers at La Fière remained under almost constant artillery and mortar fire throughout the day on June 8, but the Germans made no further attempts to get vehicles or infantry across the causeway. Later in the day, it was decided that, to break the stalemate, elements of the division would cross the inundated area just north of La Fière. The force drawing this responsibility would be Maj. Teddy H. Sanford's 1st Battalion, 325th Glider Infantry Regiment. The 325th had come in by glider beginning at 7 a.m. on D+1 (June 7) and had not yet been committed to heavy action. According to the plan, the 1st, 325th would attempt to reinforce the paratroopers isolated at Timmes' Orchard and attack south toward the western terminus of the La Fière causeway at Cauquigny. The men of the 1st, 325th crossed the flooded Merderet during the predawn hours of June 9 using an old cobblestone road referred to as "The Secret Ford." After making contact with Lieutenant Colonel Timmes' force, the glider infantrymen began their assault before first light, despite drawing fire from German soldiers in the so-called "Gray Castle," a chateau near the village of Amfreville. Moving south from the perimeter at the orchard, the battalion at first advanced steadily toward the north side of Cauquigny against sporadic resistance, but as the sun began to rise, the defenders quickly organized themselves. The German counterattack that followed overwhelmed the glidermen by sheer numbers. With concentrated automatic-weapons fire directed at them, the 325th could not maintain the momentum of the advance and began a strategic withdrawal back toward Timmes' Orchard.

Private First Class Charles N. DeGlopper of C Company, 325th Glider Infantry Regiment. During the abortive predawn assault on Cauquigny on June 9, DeGlopper walked out into the middle of Route du Hameau Flaux (present-day D15), 1,500 feet west of Cauquigny, and sprayed enemy positions with bullets from his M1918A2 Browning Automatic Rifle. Although this action provided the necessary covering fire for the withdrawal of the rest of his squad, German bullets ultimately struck DeGlopper down. He sacrificed his life to save the other members of his squad and was posthumously awarded the Medal of Honor for doing so. *National Archives and Records Administration 111-SC-313653*

When word of the failure of Major Sanford's attack on the west bank reached Major General Ridgway, 82nd Airborne Division Commanding General, he ordered a direct assault across the La Fière causeway and appointed his assistant division commander, Brig. Gen. James M. Gavin, to organize it. Gavin selected the 3rd Battalion, 325th Glider Infantry to serve as the spearhead of the attack and designated a composite company of 507th paratroopers to serve as the follow-up reserve force in the event that things went wrong for the glidermen. Leading this composite force was Capt. Robert D. Rae of Service Company, 507th.

At 10:30 a.m. on June 9, the plan was set in motion when six 155mm howitzers of the 345th Field Artillery Battalion commenced a preliminary bombardment that pounded German positions on the west bank of the Merderet. After fifteen minutes, the 155mm fire lifted, and the infantry charged in. Leading the way was Capt. John Sauls' G Company, 325th, which jumped off from a low stone wall running along the south side of the road perpendicular to the bridge and causeway. Sauls and his men ran out onto the open roadway and started down the long five hundred yards to Cauquigny. As soon as the preliminary bombardment lifted, the Germans began pouring small-arms fire into the exposed and vulnerable glidermen. Captain Sauls and a group of about thirty men made it all the way to Cauquigny, but others were not so fortunate. Lacking cover, the men of E Company, 325th and F Company, 325th began to fall, and the causeway was soon littered with the dead, the dying, and the wounded. The German machine-gun fire was of such intensity that many of the men gave in to the temptation to seek shelter along the edges of the elevated road. As the gliderman of G Company stumbled forward, stepping over the casualties scattered along the road, the assault began to bog down and lose its momentum.

Back at La Fière, it was not apparent that any elements of the 325th had made it to Cauquigny. General Gavin could only assess the situation based on what he could see, which was not encouraging. What he could see was dozens of motionless soldiers crouching along the road embankment seeking cover and dozens of dead and wounded men sprawled out in the middle of the causeway. He could not see the small groups of men struggling to hold the bridgehead. Although the situation at Cauquigny was indeed critical, to General Gavin back at La Fière, it seemed absolutely disastrous. To him, it appeared that the 325th Glider Infantry Regiment's attack had stalled and that the entire battalion was about to retreat. That is when General Gavin turned to Rae and said, "All right, you've got to go."

With that, Captain Rae led his men out onto the La Fière causeway. The company streamed across the bridge in two columns with Rae in the lead at a full sprint. As the 507th troopers passed glidermen from E Company and F Company of the 325th, they shouted to them to follow. Most of Rae's men made it all the way across and joined the 325th troopers struggling in the hedgerows at Cauquigny. The sudden arrival of Rae's company and additional 325th troopers changed the tide of the battle. Soon, the Germans were pulling back from Cauquigny in a fighting retreat toward Le Motey and Amfreville. The causeway now belonged to the 82nd Airborne Division, and the battle of La Fière had been won.

Brigadier General Gavin, the Assistant Division Commander of the 82nd Airborne Division, talks with Col. Harry L. Lewis, Commanding Officer of the 325th Glider Infantry Regiment near Etienville on June 14, 1944. These two men played central roles in the battle that unfolded over the causeway on June 9. On the left is Lt. Hugo Olson, General Gavin's aide.

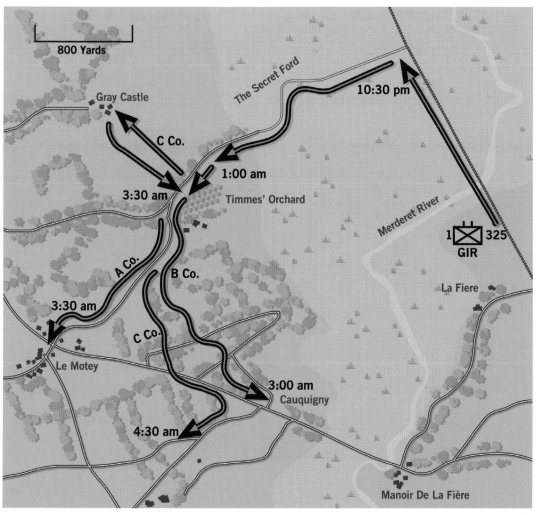

This map shows the movement of the 1st Battalion, 325th Glider Infantry Regiment during its predawn flanking maneuver on June 9, 1944. The battalion started off by proceeding north along the Carentan–Cherbourg railroad line to its crossing of the Merderet River. From there, the men continued another half mile to the point where the railroad intersects with the old Roman road running from Neuville-au-Plain to Amfreville. Known as "The Secret Ford," this cobblestone path allowed all three of the battalion's companies to cross the inundated area in only ankle-deep water. Upon reaching Timmes' Orchard, part of the battalion attacked the German outpost at the Gray Castle, while A, B, and C Companies pushed south to isolate Cauquigny and outflank the western end of the La Fière causeway.

Located two thousand feet northwest of Timmes' Orchard, this is the château that was outposted by German troops from Grenadier Regiment 1057. Because of the two turreted towers that stand on either side of the château's entrance, the men of the 82nd Airborne nicknamed the structure the "Gray Castle."

ABOVE: The ruins of Cauquigny can be seen in this photograph taken by Army historian S.L.A. Marshall shortly after the battle of the La Fière causeway. **RIGHT:** An aerial view of Cauquigny taken after the end of the war showing the heavy damage the tiny village sustained during the June 1944 battle.

Robert Dempsey Rae of Service Company, 507th as a lieutenant in 1943. Rae jumped into Normandy as a captain on D-Day and earned the Distinguished Service Cross three days later on the La Fière causeway.

ABOVE: Looking westward down the length of the La Fière causeway (present-day D15) toward Cauquigny in a view that clearly shows how the road surface is raised above the surrounding fields. Just before the invasion, the swollen Merderet River had flooded the lowlands on either side of the causeway, making it one of only two crossing points for the U.S. Army's VII Corps. When the morning attack on June 9 began to stall, soldiers from E and F Companies, 325th Glider Infantry sought cover along the edges of the causeway. The chapel at Cauquigny can be seen in the distance to the right of the road. **LEFT:** The guns of the 345th Field Artillery Battalion provided the punch behind the bombardment that preceded the attack across the La Fière causeway on June 9. Here, one of the battalion's M1 155mm howitzers is in its firing position in a field near La Fière.

Private James Schaffner of the 325th Glider Infantry Regiment poses in front of the east side of the heavily damaged chapel at Cauquigny. This photo was taken on the afternoon of June 9 after the battle had already flowed toward Le Motey. The same chapel, following repairs after the war, looks much better today.

Private Schaffner (left) and Pvt. Gerald W. Arnold (right) of the 325th Glider Infantry Regiment pose on the west side of the chapel at Cauquigny on June 9. The location looks much the same today.

The intense fighting around Cauquigny left damage that can still be observed now. Here, a U.S. .30-caliber bullet remains lodged in one of the wrought-iron bars that enclose a grave in the chapel's cemetery.

7

GRAIGNES

ALMOST FIVE THOUSAND SONS of the state of Louisiana did not return from World War II. They served in every branch of the U.S. military and fought in every theater of operations. They perished during bombing missions over Japan, were lost at sea in the mid-Atlantic, and were killed during ground combat operations in places with names like Corregidor, El Guettar, Troina, Tarawa, and Cisterna. Sons of Louisiana also lost their lives during the campaign to liberate France. This is the story of two Louisianans who paid the ultimate price during the D-Day invasion on a little hilltop in Normandy in a village called Graignes.

LEFT: An aerial view of Le Vieux Bourg (the old village) at Graignes taken from the southeast looking roughly northwest toward La Brianderie, Le Port Saint-Pierre, and Carentan. The ruins of the village's twelfth-century Roman Catholic church, now a memorial to the June 11, 1944, battle, can be clearly seen left of center in the photograph.

ABOVE: Benton J. Broussard was born in Crowley, Louisiana, in 1922 and joined the U.S. Army at Jacksonville Army Airfield in Florida on May 13, 1941. He was serving as a sergeant with the Headquarters Company, 3rd Battalion, 507th Parachute Infantry in June 1944 when the regiment jumped into Normandy. **BELOW:** Private Baragona of Service Company, 507th Parachute Infantry Regiment lost his life during the battle of Graignes on June 11, 1944.

ABOVE: George S. Baragona was born in Slidell, Louisiana, in 1919 and joined the U.S. Army at Jacksonville Army Airfield in Florida on May 30, 1941. He was serving as a private in Service Company, 507th Parachute Infantry Regiment at the time of the Normandy invasion. **BELOW:** Captain Leroy "Dave" Brummitt of the 3rd Battalion, 507th Parachute Infantry—the man who would control the tactical side of the battle of Graignes on June 11, 1944.

Benton J. Broussard was born on October 16, 1922, to a Cajun family living in the small town of Church Point in Acadia Parish, Louisiana, not far from the city of Crowley. As a child, his native tongue was French—a common reality among the people of the Atchafalaya Basin in those days. In fact, he did not begin to learn English formally until he was forced to do so in middle school. He joined the U.S. Army on May 13, 1941, at Jacksonville Army Airfield in Florida. George S. Baragona was born in the city of Slidell in St. Tammany Parish on July 24, 1919. He grew up there and went to Slidell High School where he played almost every sport offered. He was an able athlete in everything but was a star of the basketball team. After graduation, he worked for a time but eventually decided to enter the service. On May 30, 1941, he joined the U.S. Army at the same place where Broussard had enlisted just eighteen days earlier.

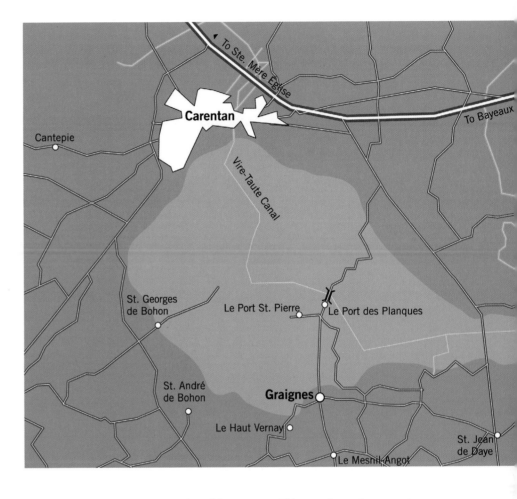

This map shows the general layout of the marshes south of Carentan. The village of Graignes can be seen five miles southeast of the city.

Both Broussard and Baragona made a critical decision after they completed basic training: they chose to join the parachute infantry. Some men did it for the "jump pay"— an extra fifty dollars paid to each paratrooper in recognition of the hazardous nature of the sky soldier's duty. Some men did it for the *esprit de corps* associated with being in an elite unit, and others did it because they assumed that the airborne would place them in combat sooner than any other army branch. In early 1942, Broussard and Baragona both graduated jump school at Fort Benning near Columbus, Georgia, after completing five qualifying, static-line jumps. They were in the right place at the right time to receive assignments to the unit that would ultimately take them to Normandy: the 507th Parachute Infantry Regiment. The army had created this new regiment in July 1942 and immediately began filling out its ranks with recently qualified personnel who were on hand at the time. Broussard was assigned to the Headquarters Company of the regiment's 3rd Battalion, while Baragona went to the regimental Service Company. The 507th remained at Fort Benning through the end of 1942 and then transferred to Alliance Army Air Field in Box Butte County, Nebraska, to prepare to go to war in North Africa. But the war there came to a conclusion in May 1943 with the surrender of Axis forces in Tunisia, and the 507th no longer had a rendezvous in the desert.

In December, Broussard and Baragona—along with the rest of the regiment—crossed the country to New York and boarded a ship bound for the United Kingdom.

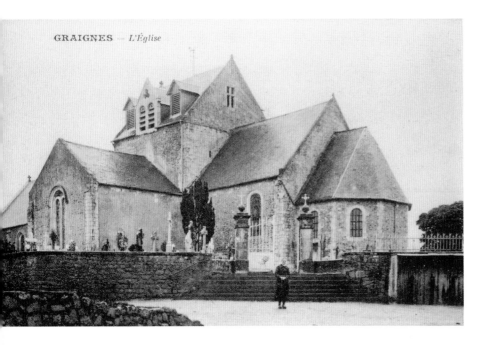

GRAIGNES — L'Église

241. - GRAIGNES. - Le Bourg

TOP: A pre-war view of the twelfth-century Roman Catholic church in Graignes. **ABOVE:** A pre-war view of the center of the village of Graignes with the twelfth-century Roman Catholic church in the background.

Once there, they trained briefly in Northern Ireland before moving to an encampment at Tollerton Hall near Grantham in Lincolnshire. The men of the 507th spent their time in England preparing for their role in the upcoming invasion of Normandy, and the training was intense. By this time, the regiment had been assigned to the 82nd Airborne Division as a temporary replacement for another regiment that had been badly bloodied during the fighting at Nettuno and Anzio in Italy. With more than two thousand physically fit, well-trained, disciplined men, and over a year's worth of constant preparation, the 507th was ready for action.

On May 28, 1944, the regiment's 2nd and 3rd Battalions were moved to and sequestered at the airfield at Barkston-Heath, where they began the final preparations for D-Day. On Monday, June 5, Broussard boarded an aircraft for the flight to Normandy: C-47 number 41-38699 from the 53rd Troop Carrier Squadron, 61st Troop Carrier Group. Baragona was on a different aircraft that evening (C-47 number 42-32919), but it was from the same squadron. Shortly before sunset, the C-47s took off and flew south as part of Mission Boston, the codename given to the operation to move the 82nd Airborne Division to Normandy. On another 53rd Troop Carrier Squadron C-47 in the same formation, the operations, plans, and training officer (S-3) for the 3rd Battalion, 507th Parachute Infantry, Capt. Leroy D. "Dave" Brummitt, was paying close attention to the trip across the English Channel. He later described the change in plans:

The Army Air Corps troop carrier squadron carrying 3rd Battalion Headquarters and Headquarters Company followed the planned flight route from England until we reached the Normandy coast, where we began to encounter German antiaircraft flak. Instead of holding course, the squadron took a different heading.

Standing in the open door of his C-47 (42-92066), Brummitt began scanning the terrain below and checking his watch starting at approximately 2:30 a.m., Tuesday, June 6, 1944. He was surprised when the red light next to the door came on moments later because he could not identify any landmarks below. Despite the fact that he had

First Lieutenant Albert L. Stephens leads Headquarters Company, 3rd Battalion, 507th on Sunday, August 23, 1943, during grand-opening festivities for the Alliance Army Airfield. Most of the men in this photograph would end up involved in the incident at Graignes. *Courtesy of the Knight Museum, Alliance, NE*

Officers from the 507th Parachute Infantry Regiment at Tollerton Hall. Kneeling: (left to right) Lt. Col. Edwin J. Ostberg, Maj. Joseph P. Fagan, Lt. Col. Arthur A. Maloney, and Lt. Col. Charles J. Timmes. Standing: (left to right) Lieutenant Colonel Kuhn, Lt. Robert M. Hennon, Capt. John J. Verret, Maj. Gordon K. Smith, Maj. Ben F. Pearson, Maj. George K. Vollmar, and Maj. Charles D. Johnston, the man who would eventually command the mixed force at Graignes. *Courtesy of Dennis and Barbara Maloney*

Staff officers of the 3rd Battalion, 507th Parachute Infantry Regiment: (left to right) Lt. H. E. Wagner, Captain Brummitt, Lt. Col. William A. Kuhn, Lt. Elmer F. Hoffman, and Lt. G. M. Dillon. *Courtesy of William D. Bowell*

Captain Loyal K. Bogart of B Company, 501st Parachute Infantry Regiment, 101st Airborne Division. He was injured on the jump and would ultimately lose his life in the battle of Graignes on June 11, 1944.

spent many long hours studying maps and aerial photographs of Normandy, Brummitt could recognize nothing. The red light indicated that he was to prepare the men to jump, but he nevertheless believed that the aircraft was not over its assigned drop zone. Brummitt checked his wristwatch again and noted that the critical planned jump time had been reached, and yet the red light continued to glow. If they were indeed over the drop zone, that light should have already changed from red to green, but this had not yet happened. "At that point I observed troopers in planes ahead of and around me leaving their planes," he later recalled. Knowing that the place for his stick of paratroopers was with the rest of the company, Brummitt had to make a split-second decision, so he shouted the "go" command and jumped. Within seconds, only the flight crew remained aboard as C-47 number 42-92066 flew away to the east and Captain Brummitt drifted toward the ground beneath an open parachute canopy. Baragona and Broussard jumped from their aircraft at approximately the same time.

Although these three C-47s had been part of Serial 25, which consisted of thirty-five aircraft, they had strayed off course alongside six other Skytrains. Because of this slight miscalculation, nine troop carrier aircraft had just dropped almost 150 paratroopers of the Headquarters Company, 3rd Battalion, 507th Parachute Infantry Regiment in the marshes south of the city of Carentan. They were supposed to have been dropped fifteen miles to the north at drop zone "T" near Amfreville, but instead they had just been given the worst misdrop of any airborne unit on June 6, 1944.

At the time of the invasion, the seasonal flooding of the Vire and Taute Rivers had produced a broad area of inundation south of Carentan. This is where Broussard,

Baragona, Brummitt, and more than one hundred others landed during the predawn hours of D-Day. At first light, they began slogging their way out of the marsh in small groups, moving toward a church on a nearby hilltop that was silhouetted by the rising sun. By 10 a.m., Captain Brummitt and twenty-five paratroopers had assembled in the village, which they soon learned was called Graignes. During the next two hours, more men climbed the hill and joined the group near the church. As a precaution, Brummitt put out perimeter security to serve as an early warning in the event that the enemy approached the village from the south, and then he made a reconnaissance of the area to the north. He was well aware that the Headquarters Company's mission required it to join the battalion with the greatest possible speed: "Otherwise the ability of the 3rd Battalion to accomplish its mission would be drastically reduced to small unit actions," as he later recalled. During his reconnaissance, Brummitt could observe no German forces between Graignes and Carentan, just 4.5 miles away across the saturated marsh of the swollen Taute River. By then he knew that the assembly area for the 82nd Airborne Division was just over the horizon to the north, and so far, everything had been quiet. Considering these circumstances, the obvious action was to move the herd toward Carentan:

> In my capacity as battalion S-3, I formulated a tentative night-march plan to go through the flooded swamp area, which we had waded, finding it to be waist to chest deep, or alternatively to go around the surrounding coastline to Carentan, link up with the U.S. force there, and continue on to the 82nd Division area.

But that plan was not executed because shortly after noon on D-Day, Maj. Charles D. Johnston, the executive officer of the 3rd Battalion, 507th Parachute Infantry, reached the hilltop. After discussing the situation with Captain Brummitt, Major Johnston took control of the 507th men assembled in the village. To him, moving the force toward the American airborne units to the north was an impractical idea because the 82nd and 101st Airborne Division drop zones were too far away. Thus, Major Johnston decided that the best course of action would be to keep the force in Graignes, organize a stronger defensive perimeter, and await a link-up with ground forces pushing inland from the landing beaches.

When the village's acting mayor, Monsieur Alphonse Voydie, learned that American paratroopers were assembling at the church, he rushed to the scene. By the time he arrived, Major Johnston had already begun the process of preparing defenses around the village. Johnston and Voydie then met to discuss the situation while Broussard translated. Without hesitating, Voydie and several other villagers told Johnston everything they could about the general layout of the area as well as the movement of nearby German troops. Because his men were going to need the ammunition and heavy weapons contained in the parachute equipment bundles that remained scattered throughout the marsh northwest of the village, Johnston asked the mayor about a boat that could be used to retrieve them. On the spot, Voydie organized several teams of villagers to begin recovering the equipment bundles and hauling them back to the Graignes perimeter. They collected bundles that contained, among other things, five MI919A4 .30-caliber

Surgeon of the 3rd Battalion, 507th Parachute Infantry Regiment Capt. Abraham Sophian, Jr. He stayed behind to care for the troopers wounded during the June 11 battle and was murdered by soldiers of the 17 SS Panzer Grenadier Division in the aftermath of the battle.

A view of the ruins of the twelfth-century Roman Catholic church at Graignes taken from just north of the village. Note that the Taute River has flooded its banks to produce a broad inundated area that comes right up to the road. The marsh was in this inundated condition near Graignes in early June 1944.
Courtesy of Paul Woodadge

machine guns and two 81mm mortars—weapons that would make the positions around the village far more defensible.

The French also recovered large quantities of ammunition that they delivered into the hands of the American defenders. Gustave Rigault was one of the citizens who assisted in this effort. From his farm at Le Port Saint-Pierre, just one mile north of Graignes, he could easily see collapsed parachutes dotting the marshy, flooded area that the French referred to as *le marais*. With the assistance of his daughters Odette (nineteen years old) and Marthe (twelve years old), he spent the afternoon of June 6 rowing out to and retrieving the U.S. equipment. While he concentrated on locating equipment bundles, the girls focused their efforts on recovering the white silk reserve parachutes that littered the area. What they hauled in from the *marais* was then deposited temporarily in a barn on the farm. That evening, two paratroopers came to Le Port Saint-Pierre to retrieve it all, but they quickly determined that the quantity was far more than they could carry. Without hesitating, Odette limbered up the family horse and cart, which was then loaded full with ammunition. She used sacks of feed and fertilizer, as well as mounds of hay, to conceal the contraband cargo—a precaution in case of an encounter with a German patrol. Odette then personally drove the cart up the hill and into Major Johnston's perimeter. According to 1st Lt. Earcle "Pip" Reed—one of the 507th officers present in Graignes—the villagers hauled in "more ammunition than we thought we could ever use." In addition to that, several field telephones, telephone wire, and a switchboard were delivered to the Americans on the hilltop.

Major Johnston also asked Mayor Voydie about the food situation. Since the misdropped troopers would almost certainly not be resupplied anytime soon, he was

ABOVE: Boats in an inundated area around Le Port Saint-Pierre near Graignes. Troopers of the 3rd Battalion, 507th Parachute Infantry Regiment landed in this marsh shortly after 2 a.m. on D-Day. *Courtesy of Odette Lelavechef* **BELOW:** Marthe and Jean Claude Rigault in their father's small boat in Le Port Saint-Pierre near Graignes. Note the inundated condition of the marsh behind them. *Courtesy of Odette Lelavechef*

ABOVE: A view from the belfry of the ruined twelfth-century Roman Catholic church in Graignes. This view is looking toward the *hippodrome* (racetrack) just south of the hilltop. The Germans attacked across the field where the track is now located during the battle on June 11, 1944. **RIGHT:** This satellite image shows the piece of topography on which Graignes is situated. The location of the village church is indicated by the white *X*. The location of the Rigault family farm at Le Port Saint-Pierre is indicated by the red *X*, and the location of the Vire-Taute Canal Bridge at Le Port des Planqués is indicated by the yellow *X*. Note that the Vire and Taute Rivers have flooded their banks to produce a broad area of inundation.

genuinely concerned about how to feed everyone. Voydie wanted to help the paratroopers, but he realized that coming up with enough to feed more than one hundred hungry men several times a day was not something that he could manage alone. He recognized that such an effort would require the cooperation and assistance of the entire community, so he called a town meeting and appealed to the citizens of Graignes to place all the resources of the village at the disposal of the Americans. The mayor must have presented convincing reasons during the meeting because there was a unanimous decision to help the paratroopers. It was a decision that was not entered into lightly, since everyone in the village knew that the penalty for being caught assisting the Americans would be swift and harsh.

After the meeting, Voydie mobilized the women of the village in an effort to procure, prepare, and distribute food for the Americans. Since the paratroopers would soon exhaust the supply of light rations they had carried with them to Normandy, something had to be done quickly. The proprietor of the village café, fifty-year-old Madame Germaine Boursier, was therefore recruited to organize an effort to provide meals to the paratroopers. Brummitt recalled that, when their rations ran out, Madame Boursier "set up a mess facility and procured foodstuffs, locally and from distant points, clandestinely transporting from the latter by cart and other concealed means." From that point forward, Madame Boursier set the standard for aiding her liberators. Under her direction, the women of Graignes began cooking around the clock so they could serve two hot meals each day. Using the café as her base of operations, she even coordinated and supervised the transportation of meals out to the soldiers occupying the many dispersed observation posts guarding the approaches to the village.

With the civilians now fully mobilized, the servicemen in the town had to adapt to an entirely new tactical situation than what they had trained for. As Brummitt recalled, Major Johnston's decision to remain in Graignes "entailed an on-the-spot reorganization of our specialist personnel into provisional infantry fire teams reinforced by the machine gun and mortar platoons." But these were not infantrymen, and this was not a rifle company. Although they had undergone "long and arduous unit training" before D-Day, that training had focused on supporting the 3rd Battalion's mission, not on direct action with the enemy. Despite that, the men took to this new assignment as if they had trained for it all along. To Brummitt, they seemed "physically and mentally ready and eager to accomplish the missions assigned." At once, the Americans went to work preparing defensive positions and digging in along a main line of resistance just 820 feet south of the church. There, Brummitt organized a series of observation posts covering the open pastures and distributed his M1919A4 Machine Guns in such a way that their fields of fire interlocked with one another. The mortar platoon dug in both tubes just south of the church cemetery and positioned two men in the church belfry. From that

Frank Naughton as a captain during the Battle of the Bulge. This photo was taken in January 1945 while the 507th was fighting in Belgium.

First Lieutenant George C. Murn, one of the officers from B Company, 501st Parachute Infantry Regiment, 101st Airborne Division who was present for the battle at Graignes on June 11, 1944.

First Lieutenant Murn of B Company/501st Parachute Infantry poses here in a B3 bomber jacket with his M1A1 Thompson submachine gun.

vantage point, the observers enjoyed an unobstructed view of the network of roads and trails leading to the village from all directions. Major Johnston established his command post in the boys' school right next door to the church while the village's defenses were being prepared. Riflemen covered the main road leading uphill to it, and a number of well-concealed antitank mines were laid to prevent vehicles from getting close. In short order, rifles, machine guns, mines, and mortars were covering all routes into Graignes.

Throughout this digging-in process, men continued to walk into the perimeter. At approximately 5:30 p.m. on D-Day, more Headquarters Company, 3rd Battalion, 507th personnel entered the village with 1st Lt. Elmer F. Farnham, 1st Lt. Lowell C. Maxwell, and the battalion's communications officer, 1st Lt. Frank Naughton. Right behind them was a group of troopers from B Company, 501st Parachute Infantry Regiment, 101st Airborne Division led by Capt. Loyal K. Bogart, whose legs had been injured during the jump. When he reported in at Graignes, he insisted that he was still capable of helping and asked for something to do. Major Johnston placed him in charge of the central switchboard at the command post in the boys' school. The remaining B Company, 501st men were given a sector on the line. Two other 101st Airborne troopers, Pfc. Norwood H. Lester and Pfc. George A. Brown, also joined the group on D-Day, but they were not from the 501st. These two men belonged to B Battery of the 81st Airborne Anti-Aircraft/Anti-Tank Battalion, and they had landed in the marsh shortly after 4 a.m. on the 6th, but not by parachute. Lester and Green had been passengers on board Waco CG-4A number 43-41826, a glider piloted that night by 2nd Lt. Irwin J. Morales and 2nd Lt. Thomas O. Ahmad of the 74th Troop Carrier Squadron, 434th Troop Carrier Group. Waco number 43-41826 had been assigned the slot "Chalk 42" of Mission Chicago, the pre-dawn glider assault by elements of the 101st Airborne. Chalk 42 was supposed to have landed ten miles north on Landing Zone W near Hiesville alongside fifty-one other gliders, but instead it came down northwest of Graignes near a cluster of buildings known as La Brianderie. Captain Brummitt placed Second Lieutenant Morales in charge of the right-flank outpost of the line defending the hilltop, and Second Lieutenant Ahmad was given responsibility for a group of men near the church.

On June 9, two soldiers from the 29th Infantry Division who had been separated from their unit walked into the

ABOVE: An aerial view of Le Vieux Bourg at Graignes taken from the southeast looking roughly northwest toward La Brianderie, Le Port Saint-Pierre, and Carentan. The ruins of the village's twelfth-century Roman Catholic church, now a memorial to the June 11, 1944, battle, can be clearly seen in the center of the photograph. **BELOW:** A post-battle view of the exterior of the twelfth-century Roman Catholic church in Graignes showing damage to the structure sustained during the fighting on June 11, 1944.

RIGHT: A post-battle view of the exterior of the twelfth-century Roman Catholic church in Graignes showing damage to the structure sustained during the fighting on June 11, 1944. BELOW: Two views of the nave of the twelfth-century Roman Catholic church in Graignes taken before and after the battle of June 11, 1944.

perimeter, giving fleeting hope to the idea that forces advancing inland from the beaches would soon link up with the mixed group of Americans on the hilltop. But other nationalities also became part of the defensive force at Graignes. A pair of Spaniards who had escaped from a nearby German forced-labor camp emerged from the marsh and climbed the hill. They could both speak French, so they made a great contribution. Then Flight Sgt. Stanley Kevin Black of the Royal Australian Air Force arrived. A bombardier in RAF No. 106 Squadron, Black's Lancaster (NE 150) had been badly damaged during a raid over Caen during the night of June 6 and 7. The bomber managed to limp approximately twenty miles northeast before finally crashing between the towns of Saint-Jean-de-Daye and Saint-Fromond. Flight Sergeant Black parachuted to safety that night and was then taken by the French to Graignes because Allied troops were known to be there.

During the three days that followed, Allied troops in the village manned outposts around the clock, adjusted protective fire around the hilltop, and fine-tuned pre-sighted mortars. They established wire communications between various dispersed positions around Graignes, prepared fallback positions, and generally made ready to contact the enemy. Throughout these preparations, "the officers and men proved beyond a doubt that they were elite troops of the highest order," as Captain Brummitt later described. By June 9, the assembled group in the village numbered 182 (12 officers and 170 enlisted). None of them had yet experienced combat with the enemy, but that would soon change.

On June 10, elements of the 17 SS Panzer Grenadier Division "Götz von Berlichingen" moved into the area around Graignes, setting the stage for battle. When the invasion began on June 6, the 17 SS was positioned 163 miles to the south near the city of Thouars in the Deux-Sèvres department of western France, but the unit quickly received orders to join the developing battle in Normandy. To make the move, the division's six battalions were divided into four marschgruppe (movement groups) that made use of parallel axes of advance over the road network leading to the area around the city of Carentan. SS Panzergrenadier Regiment 38 formed Marschgruppe 2, and Graignes was directly in its path of advance. On Saturday, June 10, a mechanized reconnaissance patrol from Marschgruppe 2 (16 SS Panzergrenadier Regiment 38) approached a section of the main defensive line that was under the command of 1st Lt. George C. Murn from B Company, 501st Parachute Infantry Regiment, 101st Airborne Division. Murn's men let the patrol get close and then opened fire, killing four of the enemy. Simultaneously, another element of Marschgruppe 2 outflanked Graignes to the east by moving up the road running from

First Lieutenant Lowell C. Maxwell would also lose his life in the June 11, 1944, battle.

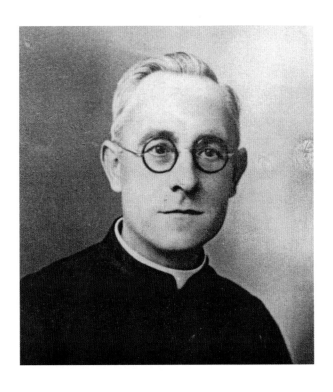

Father Albert Leblastier—one of the priests murdered at Graignes by panzergrenadiers of 17 SS in the aftermath of the battle of June 11, 1944.

Saint-Jean-de-Daye to Carentan. As they did so, another patrol followed the length of what is now D89 to approach Graignes from the north, using the bridge across the Vire-Taute Canal at Le Port des Planqués. There, a single five-hundred-meter-long causeway permitted vehicular traffic to cross the inundated area north of the village, but it was being guarded by a detachment of 507th paratroopers under the command of First Lieutenant Naughton. After a brief exchange of fire with the SS panzergrenadiers, the Americans blew the bridge and pulled back to the hilltop.

That night, the outposts reported hearing activity south of Graignes, and they made contact with the Germans several times. The knowledge that a significant German force was out in the hedgerows sent a wave of nervousness through the Americans, who spent the night on full alert, with officers conducting almost constant inspections of the perimeter. Before this, the paratroopers at Graignes had been confident that American units to the north would get through to them before the enemy could launch any kind of serious attack against their perimeter. But the crescendo of enemy activity around the village on June 10 seemed to indicate they could not expect relief to arrive in time. To the American paratroopers and the French civilians in Graignes, the moment of truth was close at hand.

There was no sign of the enemy, and all was quiet the next morning (June 11), the first Sunday since the invasion began. Major Johnston gave permission for some of the men to attend mass. Marthe and Odette Rigault went to mass that morning as well, arriving just as the parish priest, sixty-four-year-old Father Albert Leblastier, began the liturgy. Just ten minutes later, gunfire interrupted the service. Captain Brummitt heard firing south of the village, rushed to the scene, and quickly determined that a large German force was approaching Graignes. He shifted some of his men to reinforce the southern flank and prepared to receive the weight of a direct attack. Back in the church, a woman burst into the sanctuary yelling "The Germans are coming!" and causing a panic among the assembled parishioners and soldiers. During the brief gun battle, all of the villagers assembled for mass sheltered inside the nave. It was all over in less than fifteen minutes. A patrol element from SS Panzergrenadier Regiment 38's 1st Battalion had probed the village's defensive line, causing the Americans to reveal some of their positions. As soon as the fight was over, Major Johnston ordered Brummitt to place all available personnel on the defensive line below the village. He recognized that another assault would soon follow.

At about 2 p.m., the I SS Panzergrenadier Regiment 38 commenced a light bombardment of Graignes. The fire came from either the infamous Model 34 80mm mortar (8cm Granatwerfer 34), a weapon organic to every German infantry company during World War II, or the Model 18 75mm light infantry howitzer (7.5cm leichtes infanteriegeschütz 18), a weapon that was definitely part of SS Panzergrenadier Regiment 38's table of equipment. The preparatory fire was swiftly followed by a second infantry assault against the flanks of the southern defensive line. Although the attackers moved so swiftly that the perimeter was almost breached, Captain Brummitt quickly shifted forces to meet the threat, and the line held. During this phase of the battle, the paratroopers unleashed supporting fire of their own through the effective use of their two M1 81mm mortars. With observers in the church tower providing fire direction, the Americans enjoyed a

Five-year-old Phillip Hoffman poses here with his older brother, Richard, at the family home in Elkhart, Indiana, in 1943. Richard had recently completed airborne school and would soon be assigned to the 501st Parachute Infantry Regiment, 101st Airborne Division. In less than a year, he would meet his death at the hands of members of SS Panzergrenadier Regiment 38, 17 SS at the village of Le Mesnil Angot near Graignes. This was the last time the two brothers would be together. *Courtesy of Phillip Hoffman*

Private First Class Richard Jacob Hoffman of the Headquarters Company, 1st Battalion, 501st Parachute Infantry Regiment, 101st Airborne Division. He was executed by members of SS Panzergrenadier Regiment 38, 17 SS Panzer Grenadier Division at the conclusion of the battle of Graignes on June 11, 1944. *Courtesy of Phillip Hoffman*

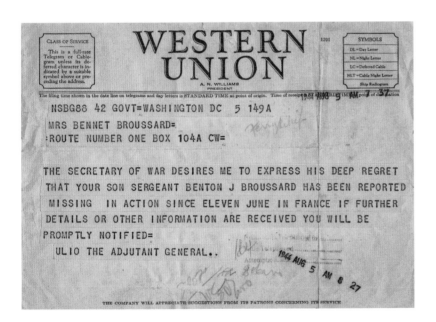

The telegram that reached Sgt. Benton J. Broussard's mother on August 5, 1944, notifying her that he had been listed as "missing in action" after the battle of Graignes. She would soon be notified of his death.

Edouard and Odette Lelavechef married on October 6, 1945, which is when this photograph was taken. Odette's wedding gown was made from the white silk of the 507th reserve parachutes that she recovered from the marsh near their family farm on D-Day. *Courtesy of Odette Lelavechef*

Four post-battle views of the exterior of the twelfth-century Roman Catholic church in Graignes showing damage to the structure sustained during the fighting on June 11, 1944.

crucial advantage. The cumulative effect of the mortar fire, the crossfire of the machine guns, and accurate rifle fire disrupted the attack to such a degree that the Germans eventually broke it off.

Although the line had held for a second time that day, the paratroopers and the citizens of Graignes began to suffer their first casualties. The church sanctuary soon became a busy place as the wounded received medical attention there from the 3rd Battalion, 507th Medical Detachment, a portion of which flew and jumped with the Headquarters Company to provide direct medical support in the field. The detachment was under the command of twenty-nine-year-old Capt. Abraham Sophian, Jr., and included several medics from the 507th and the 501st. Father Leblastier and Father Louis Lebarbanchon, a thirty-two-year-old former pupil temporarily in Graignes to recuperate from tuberculosis, provided comfort to the wounded soldiers and to several villagers.

An uneasy quiet fell over Graignes following the second attack. During this lull, Captain Brummitt checked the line and found that mortar and small-arms ammunition levels were beginning to run low. The remainder was then redistributed among the defenders to provide each position with an even supply. While this was being done, an unnerving sound rose from the maze of hedgerows south of the village. The grind of heavy vehicular movement announced that the Germans were bringing in reinforcements. Major Johnston then sent all of the civilians away, since the evidence indicated that Graignes was about to be the target of a major attack. After almost nine hours of confinement in the church during the day's fighting, Marthe and Odette were both ready to leave. Marthe remembered that, "At 7 o'clock p.m. Major Johnston told us that we should go home because they did not have enough ammunition for the night." The two sisters then slipped out of the village and returned safely to Le Port Saint-Pierre.

From the hilltop the signs grew more ominous with each passing hour. Through his binoculars, First Lieutenant Reed could see two German artillery pieces being set up near a farm at Thieuville one mile south of the church. SS Panzergrenadier Regiment 38 included several heavy-weapons sections armed with different types of guns that could have provided fire support for the battle. First of all, 2 SS Artillerie Regiment 17 was armed with the Model 18 105mm light field howitzer (10.5cm leichte Feld Haubitze 18). Then there was SS Panzerjäger Abteilung 17, which was armed with the potent and deadly Model 40 75mm antitank gun (7.5cm Panzer Abwehr Kanone 40). Finally, there was 3 SS Artillerie Regiment 17, which was armed with the most powerful weapon in the regiment: the Model 33 150mm heavy infantry gun (15cm schweres Infanterie Geschütz 33). Although it remains unclear what type they were, at about 7 p.m., the two guns at Thieuville opened fire on Graignes, and incoming rounds quickly swept across the buildings clustered on top of the hill. As it began, "Pip" Reed looked up at the belfry just in time to see it take a direct hit. The enemy shell ripped through the observation post, killing First Lieutenant Farnham and another soldier.

The artillery barrage was the beginning of the final assault against the Americans at Graignes. After a thorough "softening up" of the objective, troops from I SS Panzergrenadier Regiment 38 moved in for the *coup de grace*. To the defenders on the hilltop, it was immediately obvious that this assault force was significantly larger than the

one from the afternoon battle. With the observation post in the belfry destroyed, it was no longer possible to deliver mortar fire with any degree of accuracy. As the enemy crept closer, the mortar crewmen cranked the elevation of their tubes to the maximum in a desperate attempt to prevent being overrun, but it was of no use. Attacking SS panzergrenadiers closed ranks with the defensive perimeter in the village, and, as darkness settled over Graignes, the Germans resumed their relentless drive toward the hilltop.

By the time the Germans made the final thrust into Graignes that night, the defensive perimeter south of the village had been reduced to a few isolated pockets of resistance. Defenders began to run out of ammunition, and the enemy quickly exploited the situation by overrunning their positions. Those points of the line not overrun were cut off from communication with the command post and the aid station. Major Johnston had Captain Brummitt pull his remaining outposts back to a defensive line closer to the village. As he attempted to make contact with each point along the line, Brummitt became involved in several intense firefights. When the enemy began to outflank the last position, he ordered the crewmembers of the remaining M1919A4 .30-caliber Light Machine Gun to withdraw to a previously designated fallback position. Just as the machine gunner and assistant machine gunner started to move, German rifle fire killed them both. Without hesitating, Captain Brummitt dropped his M1A1 Carbine and scooped up the M1919A4 machine gun and its box of ammunition but left behind the weapon's M2 tripod because it had been damaged. He then leaped over a nearby stone wall that two other troopers were using for protection while providing covering fire. As he reached their side of the wall, German small-arms fire killed both of the other troopers as well. Brummitt swung the machine gun around, steadied it on top of the wall, and fired a burst in the direction of the enemy fire. After that, he "heard no more from that sector."

When Brummitt returned to the hilltop area near the command post, Battalion Sergeant Major Robert Salewski informed him that Major Johnston had given the order to abandon the position and attempt to return individually to friendly lines. At about that time, one final artillery concentration fell on the hilltop, this time targeting the boys' school. The shells battered the stone building, violently hurling fragments and rock in every direction. One of those rounds crashed into the roof directly above the room that Captain Bogart and Major Johnston occupied. When it exploded, the walls collapsed in on both men. Even more fire from the barrage then landed on the building, killing some and sending others running for better cover. Broussard, who had been functioning as the major's translator since the invasion began and had therefore been part of the staff around the command post the entire six days, made a dash for the protection of the heavily damaged church. He only had to cover two hundred feet to make it to the main entrance of the sanctuary, but he did not quite get there. One of the incoming artillery

The plaque reads:

GRAIGNES

AUBRIL Louise
DEFORTESCU Adrien
DUJARDIN Eugénie
FOLLIOT Isidore
FOLLIOT Georges
FRANÇOISE Lucien
GIRARD Eugénie
LEBARBANCHON Charles A...
LEBLASTIER Albert H...
LECONTE Marguerite
LEDOLLEY Edouard
LEFRANC Marcel
LERECULEY Marie Louise
LEROSIER Rosalie
LESCALIER Aline
LETRESOR Émile
LUCE André

MARIE Auguste
MARTIN Germaine
MARTIN Jules son époux
MAUGER Albert
MIGNOT Octave
MOSQUERON Ernest
PALLA Désiré
PERRETTE Joseph
PEZERIL Madeleine
RIGAULT Louis
THEREZE Louis
VARDON Louis
BAZIRE Louis

LE MESNIL ANGOT

PEZERIL Paulette
TURPIN Georges

PARACHUTISTES AMÉRICAINS
MORTS
POUR LA LIBÉRATION
DE GRAIGNES
JUIN 1944

LOVE William
COLLABAM Ray M.
PARKLOM Leop.
ROCHWELL Robert R.
NOFF James
BARAGONA Georges
PITTIS Edward J.
STACHONIAN Joseph
MARTINEZ Arnald J.
BOUSSARD Berton J.
CHOQUETTE Walte J.
CASAS Jesus

ABOVE: Alphonse Voydie (left) shakes hands with Frank Juliano (right) during the dedication ceremony for the first plaque at the Graignes memorial site in 1946. Voydie was the acting mayor of Graignes in June 1944, and Juliano was a Private First Class in B Company of the 501st Parachute Infantry Regiment, 101st Airborne Division during the battle. **OPPOSITE:** Juliano inspects the original plaque at Graignes shortly after its dedication in 1946. Following the battle of June 11, 1944, Juliano hid for several weeks in a large oven in an outbuilding on a farm known as Le Rotz on the outskirts of Graignes.

The twelfth-century Roman Catholic church in Graignes as it looks today. It is now a memorial to the battle that took place in the village on June 11, 1944.

rounds caught him in the open and killed him just steps away from the church door.

Once darkness had fallen, it was clear that the paratroopers would not be able to hold on much longer. Captain Brummitt learned that Major Johnston had been killed, and command of what was left of the force at Graignes devolved to him. With the Germans swarming toward the center of the village, the American tactical situation in Graignes had fallen apart at the seams once and for all. Realizing that the enemy attack would most likely resume at dawn and that their chances of survival would be slim if they remained in the area, Captain Brummitt decided that the time had come to evacuate. Still carrying the .30-caliber machine gun and ammunition can, he ordered Sergeant Salewski to round up everyone left on the hilltop. After assembling all the men who could be located, it appeared that they were the last remaining members of Headquarters Company, 3rd Battalion, 507th in the village. Brummitt led the entire group away toward the designated assembly area. The defenders had done everything in their power to hold out, but in the end, a numerically superior enemy attacking with supporting fire simply overwhelmed them. An entry in 17 SS Panzer Grenadier Division's *kriegstagebuch* (war diary) later ominously recorded this summary:

> *Graignes würde am 11.6 23,30 genommen, das Gelände im Laufe der Nacht vom 11.-12.6 gesäubert.*

Graignes was taken at 11:30 p.m. on June 11. The area was cleaned out during the course of the night of the 11th and 12th of June.

Although Captain Brummitt was unaware of it at the time, a number of personnel did not depart the hilltop when he ordered the evacuation. Captain Sophian, his medics, and a group of wounded troopers were unintentionally left behind in the church. "Had I been aware of this situation, I would have made a specific move to bring them along," Brummitt later said. It remains unknown whether or not Captain Sophian received Major Johnston's order to withdraw or if he chose to remain behind with the expectation that his men and the wounded would be treated as prisoners of war. Those details do not matter much considering what happened next. At the end of the final assault, the men of I SS Panzergrenadier Regiment 38 stormed the church and found Captain Sophian's aid station. They then forced the captain and

The memorial site at Graignes includes a new plaque that lists the names of some of the U.S. soldiers who lost their lives there during the battle of June 11, 1944.

The final resting place of Sergeant Broussard in Woodlawn Cemetery in Crowley, Louisiana. He was killed in action during the battle at Graignes on June 11, 1944.

all of the wounded outside where they were divided into two groups and marched away from the church. One group (nine troopers) was marched off to the south, and the other group (five troopers) was marched down to the edge of a shallow pond behind Madame Boursier's café. At the edge of the pond, the Germans bayoneted the wounded men and dumped them into the water. The other group of 507th paratroopers was forced to march two miles south to a field near the village of Le Mesnil-Angot. There, the nine men were shot and then buried in shallow graves.

When I SS Panzergrenadier Regiment 38 took prisoners on the hilltop at the end of the battle, three of those prisoners were officers. Captain Sophian was captured unwounded in his aid station, and Captain Bogart and Major Johnston were pulled, wounded but still alive, from the rubble of the boys' school. All three were taken three miles southwest to the village of Tribehou, where they were interrogated for several hours and then executed. Their bodies were dumped along the Route de la Terrette (present-day D57). Major Johnston's remains were not found until after the war. But the execution of paratroopers was not the end of the brutal retaliation that followed the conclusion of the battle at Graignes. Once in control of the hilltop, 17 SS troops proceeded to the rectory to exact punishment. They knew that the church's belfry had been used throughout the battle as an observation post, and they went looking for the people who had allowed it. When they found Father Leblastier and Father Lebarbanchon in their quarters, they dragged them into the courtyard and shot them both to death.

Despite the violent battle, the brutal execution of U.S. prisoners, and the murder of the two French priests, more than one hundred paratroopers made it out alive. Captain Brummitt's group of troopers crossed the *marais* without incident that night and took up concealed positions in a hedgerow south of Carentan shortly before dawn on June 12. Soon thereafter, another group, led by Capt. Richard H. Chapman and First Lieutenant Naughton, joined them, bringing the total number to eighty troopers from 3rd Battalion, 507th Parachute Infantry Regiment; seven from B Company, 501st Parachute Infantry Regiment, 101st Division; two Spaniards; and one French citizen. They reached the safety of U.S. lines the following morning. Several smaller groups of paratroopers who became separated from the others in the pitch darkness ultimately found their way to Carentan during the days that followed, and some even remained hidden in the village, avoiding capture. It is known that several paratroopers hid in the attic of the old girls' school and that one man even spent the next several weeks concealed in a large oven in an outbuilding on a farm known as Le Rotz. This man, Pfc. Frank Juliano of B Company, 501st Parachute Infantry remained in the oven by day and lived off of collected apples at night. Although he did not starve, he did not eat like a king either. Juliano rejoined the 501st after ground troops finally reached Graignes in late July.

The village's citizens became refugees soon after the battle when the German military forced everyone to evacuate the area. They eventually returned in August only to find that their town was permanently touched by war. What happened to Graignes in 1944 is commemorated today with two street names: the main stretch of D89 going through town is now known as *Rue de 11 Juin 1944* (Street of June 11, 1944), and the road leading up the hill to the church memorial has been renamed *Rue de 507e R.I.P.* (Street of the

The final resting place of Sergeant Baragona in Our Lady of Lourdes Cemetery in Slidell, Louisiana. He was a private in Service Company, 507th Parachute Infantry Regiment and lost his life during the battle of Graignes on June 11, 1944.

507th Parachute Infantry Regiment). After the war, town leaders eventually chose to build a new place of worship at the bottom of the hill where D89 intersects with D57. They also chose to convert the heavily damaged ruins of the old church into a memorial dedicated to the memory of those who lost their lives in the village in 1944. At the heart of the memorial site, the final resting place of Father Leblastier and Father Lebarbanchon is a crypt directly beneath the crossing, inscribed with the words *Fusilles par les Allemands le 12 Juin 1944* (Shot by the Germans on June 12, 1944). In the area where the choir and the high altar used to be, a black granite plaque bears the names of the French civilians and U.S. paratroopers whose lives ended during the battle. On that plaque's center column, the names Benton Broussard and George Baragona are, coincidentally, one above the other. The army recovered their bodies more than a month after the battle and then interred them at the temporary American cemetery on Omaha Beach at Saint-Laurent-sur-Mer. After the war, the families of both men were given the option of either having their remains permanently buried overseas or having them returned to the United States. When both families chose repatriation, Broussard and Baragona were brought home to Louisiana. Today, Broussard rests in Woodlawn Cemetery in the city of Crowley beneath a headstone that incorrectly lists him as having served in the 17th Airborne Division. Although the 507th Parachute Infantry ultimately served in the 17th Airborne Division later in the war, the regiment belonged to the 82nd Airborne Division when Broussard served in it during the Normandy campaign. At the time of his death, he wore an 82nd Airborne Division patch on his left shoulder.

Baragona lies buried in his hometown of Slidell in Our Lady of Lourdes Cemetery beneath a custom headstone that incorrectly lists his date of death as June 6, 1944. In actuality, he survived D-Day and the five days that followed, only to be struck down by shell fragments during the same artillery bombardment that killed Broussard. Baragona's headstone is decorated with a pair of airborne jump wings and the inscription "Lest We Forget." These two sons of Louisiana went to France in 1944 and lost their lives on the hilltop at Graignes. They may not be household names, but they are not forgotten.

AFTER-MATH

The Storm

On June 19, 1944, the worst storm in forty years struck Normandy and pounded the coast for three days, finally abating on June 22. With heavy rain, howling wind, and violent surf, this massive storm system damaged both of the temporary Mulberry harbors the Allies had built to support landing operations. The British Mulberry Harbor at Arromanches, nicknamed "Port Winston," sustained light damage, but it was ultimately repaired and continued to serve. The American Mulberry Harbor on Omaha Beach at Vierville-sur-Mer, on the other hand, sustained such heavy damage that it could not be repaired. Everything that came ashore in the American sector from that point onward was landed across the open beach by LSTs and other landing craft. A sobering point about this storm relates

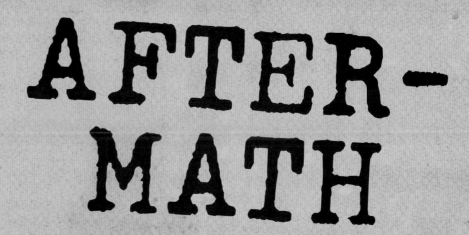

LEFT: These Germans are not actually German but Polish volunteers captured near Utah Beach being guarded by sailors from the 2nd Naval Beach Battalion on June 15, 1944. The sailor on the left is armed with an M1903 rifle. The older prisoner is wearing M42 ankle boots and leggings (what the Germans called *schnürschuhe und gamaschen*), while the younger one wears hobnailed Model 1939 jackboots (*knobelbecher*). U.S. Navy photograph, now in the collections of the U.S. National Archives 80-G-253030

ABOVE: This photograph of Omaha Beach was taken in the vicinity of the Ruquet Valley/Exit E-1 looking to the east down the length of the Easy Red sector during the third week of June 1944. A large assortment of military equipment can be seen on the shingle in this view, including a Bantam T-3 trailer and several beached LCVPs. In the center, LCT-1035 is easily identified by the distinctive paint scheme and hull markings unique to the Royal Navy.

BELOW: This view shows low tide at the Easy Red sector of Omaha Beach in front of the Ruquet River Valley. Here, the cameraman is facing to the northwest and has captured beach obstacles, landing craft, a pair of U.S. Army small tugs, and "corncob" blockships of "Gooseberry 2" for the American Mulberry Harbor (in the background). There are two LCVPs from the *Crescent City*–class attack transport USS *Charles Carroll* (APA-28) in the foreground, one sitting on its keel and the other upturned.

back to General Eisenhower's decision to postpone the invasion from June 5 to 6. Some of the officers on the Supreme Headquarters Allied Expeditionary Force staff felt that the safer bet would be to wait until later in the month. Had General Eisenhower elected to postpone the invasion by three weeks instead of twenty-four hours, the landings would have occurred during this storm with potentially catastrophic results.

Not a Harbor, But a Field of Ruins

The U.S. Army's VII Corps, comprising eighty thousand men, was given the mission of landing on Utah Beach, attacking toward and eventually capturing the sprawling port facility at Cherbourg. After cutting off the Cotentin Peninsula on June 16, VII Corps forces turned to the north and began pushing toward the city, with the 9th Infantry Division, the 79th Infantry Division, and the 4th Infantry Division as the spearhead. Some German commanders wanted to withdraw fighting forces from Normandy to mount a more effective defense of occupied France, but *Führer und Reichskanzler* Adolf Hitler rejected that proposition in his meeting with *Generalfeldmarschall* Gerd von Rundstedt and *Generalfeldmarschall* Erwin Rommel at the Führerhauptquartier Wolfsschlucht 2 in the city of Margival, France, near Soissons on June 17. In that meeting, Hitler instructed the commander of German forces in Cherbourg, *Generalleutnant* Karl-Wilhelm von Schlieben, to hold out, "Even if worse comes to worst." He went on to instruct von Schlieben with these fateful words: "It is your duty to defend the last bunker and leave to the enemy not a harbor but a field of ruins. . . . The German people and the whole world are watching your fight; on it depends the conduct and result of operations to smash the beachheads, and the honor of the German Army and of your own name." The U.S. attack on the city

A dead U.S. soldier lies on the shingle in front of the Les Moulins Draw/Exit D-3 on the Easy Green sector of Omaha Beach on Wednesday, June 7, 1944. The three-story house behind him is Villa les Sables d'Or, which provided cover the day before for a fifty-man force under the command of Major Bingham, commander of the 2nd Battalion, 116th Infantry Regiment. The cleanup of Omaha Beach has not yet begun at this point, and the dead still litter the battlefield.

ABOVE LEFT: The body of a young U.S. Army soldier lies face down in the sand at the base of an obstacle on Omaha Beach. He was killed during the intense fighting in front of Vierville-sur-Mer on D-Day, and the tide carried his body to the Dog White sector overnight, where this photograph was taken during the morning low tide on Wednesday, June 7, 1944. The fact that he is wearing M1942 HBT trousers and an M1941 Field Jacket suggests that he was a Ranger either from the 2nd or 5th Battalion. He still wears his M1926 Inflatable Lifebelt, and two weapons lay in the sand at his feet: one is an M1 Garand semiautomatic rifle, and the other is an M1903 Springfield bolt-action rifle. He was just one of the almost nine hundred soldiers of the U.S. Army's V Corps to lose his life during the battle of Omaha Beach. *U.S. Coast Guard Collection in the U.S. National Archives 26-G-2397* **ABOVE RIGHT:** Another GI who did not survive the battle of Omaha Beach is seen here during the morning low tide on June 7. He still wears his M1926 Inflatable Lifebelt, an M7 Assault Gas Mask Bag, an M1941 Field Jacket, and M1937 Olive Drab Wool Field Trousers. A wedding ring is on his left ring finger, so a young woman back home became a widow on D-Day.

Dodge WC-54 3/4-ton ambulances from the 546th Medical Ambulance Company land on the Easy Red sector of Omaha Beach from LCT-550 on Monday, June 12, 1944. The lead ambulance is equipped with an extended air intake/snorkel for fording deep water. The 546th was one of the most important companies supporting the U.S. Army's XIX Corps during combat operations in Normandy. *National Archives and Records Administration/U.S. Army Signal Corps 111-SC-191168*

began on June 22 with a massive aerial and artillery bombardment. The fighting continued on the 24th, and von Schlieben dutifully passed on Hitler's instruction "defend to the last cartridge" to his garrison force. On June 25, a massive naval bombardment made it possible for the Americans to enter the downtown waterfront area. On June 26, soldiers from the U.S. 39th Infantry Regiment, 9th Infantry Division captured von Schlieben himself in the city's Saint-Sauveur neighborhood, marking the end of organized opposition. Although the harbor forts and the old French naval arsenal did not surrender until June 29, the battle was over. U.S. forces had seized the port and captured thirty thousand German troops.

Saint-Lô

After establishing the beachhead in the American sectors of the invasion area, the U.S. First Army moved on to the next phase of operations. This called for three U.S. Army corps to push south from Carentan as part of the drive to continue expanding the beachhead. Directly in the path of the Army's XIX Corps was the crucially important crossroads town of Saint-Lô. As the Germans began to recover and reorganize in the aftermath of the June 6 landings, they established a heavily reinforced line of resistance just north of the city that made use of terrain favoring the defense. The principal terrain feature encountered there was known as *bocage* to the French and simply as "hedgerows" to the American soldiers who had to fight among them. When the XIX Corps approached Saint-Lô at the beginning of July, it quickly bogged down before the difficult terrain and the stiff resistance. The fighting that followed included intense artillery duels and carpet-bombing that destroyed as much as 95 percent of the city. The extent of the damage earned Saint-Lô the unenviable nickname "The Capital of the Ruins."

With U.S. forces brought to a standstill in front of Saint-Lô toward the end of July, a general breakthrough in the area was needed. Accordingly, an operation named Cobra was planned for the area immediately west of the city for July 24. Before Cobra's kickoff, though, a corridor just north of the towns of Saint-Gilles and Marigny was carpet-bombed in order to weaken the German defensive lines in front of the U.S. 30th Infantry Division. Although bombs accidentally fell on friendly positions, even resulting in the death of Lt. Gen. Lesley J. McNair on July 25, the carpet-bombing

ABOVE: German Army soldiers from 709 Infanterie Division come forward to surrender on June 9 at Taret de Ravenoville, five miles up the coast from Utah Beach. The eastern shore of the Cotentin Peninsula south of Quinéville was cleared by troops of the 22nd Infantry Regiment, 4th Infantry Division and the 39th Infantry Regiment, 9th Infantry Division during the first week of the invasion. *National Archives and Records Administration/U.S. Army Signal Corps 111-SC-190259*

BELOW: Troops from the 4th Infantry Division lead German Army soldiers from 709 Infanterie Division to a prisoner-of-war enclosure on Utah Beach on June 6, 1944. *National Archives and Records Administration/U.S. Army Signal Corps 111-SC-190463*

On Monday, June 12, 1944, several high-ranking U.S. military leaders landed at the Ruquet Valley from a DUKW for a brief inspection tour of the Omaha Beach area. Here, Adm. Alan G. Kirk (closest to the camera) is letting himself down from the side of the DUKW with U.S. Army Chief of Staff George Marshall right behind him. General Eisenhower has just planted his left foot on the PSP used to provide a stable surface for vehicular traffic driving up Exit E-1. Looking down on General Eisenhower, General Arnold leans over the gunwale of the DUKW. *National Archives and Records Administration/U.S. Army Signal Corps 111-SC-190238*

successfully opened a gap in the German lines. The U.S. 2nd and 3rd Armored Divisions then pushed southwest from the Saint-Lô area with such swiftness that the Germans were caught off balance. By July 31, the U.S. Army's XIX Corps had destroyed the last forces opposing Bradley's First Army. Finally freed from the hedgerows, once American mechanized units began moving quickly, they were practically unstoppable. Operation Cobra transformed the bogged-down, attritional infantry combat of Normandy into the rapid, maneuver warfare that eventually led to the creation of the Falaise Pocket.

Mortain

Following the breakout's success, units of the U.S. First Army streamed southward toward the city of Avranches. On August 1, General Patton's Third Army went into action for the first time and began to operate in the area south of the city, but the U.S. Army held only a very narrow corridor. In an attempt to cut off Patton's Army, Hitler personally ordered a counteroffensive to sever the corridor linking the Third Army with Allied forces to the north. Called Operation Lüttich, this German attack called for the XXXXVII Panzerkorps (47th Panzer Corps) to push west from the area around the city of Mortain toward Avranches. If they could recapture Avranches, they could trap the Third Army and trigger an American retreat. Consisting of one and a half SS Panzer Divisions and two German Army Panzer Divisions, the Lüttich assault force began to advance on August 7. The 2 SS Panzer Division "Das Reich" moved so swiftly at first that it easily surrounded the 2nd Battalion of the U.S. 120th Infantry Regiment on Hill 314 near Mortain. By August 13, Allied air strikes had taken their toll on the German advance, and they had been driven back with the loss of 150 tanks. The German counteroffensive had failed to stem the U.S. advance as Hitler envisioned, and it set the stage for what would soon happen south of Caen.

Le Dénouement

In the aftermath of the failure of the German Mortain counteroffensive, Patton's Third Army made rapid advances to the south and southeast. General Bernard Law Montgomery's 21st Army Group then struck southeastward from Caen in two back-to-back operations: Totalize and Tractable. The advancing Western Allies thereafter encircled the German Seventh and Fifth Panzer Armies during the second week of August in a pocket between the cities of Chambois and Falaise. By the evening of August 21, the pocket was closed with around fifty thousand German troops trapped inside. Although a significant number managed to escape, German losses were huge, and the Allies had achieved a decisive victory that resulted in the destruction of the bulk of German forces west of the Seine River, opening the way to Paris and bringing Operation Overlord to an end.

ABOVE: Captured in the battle of Saint-Lô, German Army and Luftwaffe prisoners are gathered on Utah Beach for transfer to England for internment. The group includes Poles, Austrians, and Czechs in addition to ethnic Germans. LST-21, a Coast Guard–manned landing ship, is waiting in the background to take them aboard, and a VLA antiaircraft barrage balloon floats above. *U.S. Coast Guard Collection in the U.S. National Archives 26-G-0710441* **BELOW:** A column of lucky German prisoners of war being marched out to a waiting LST across the sands of Utah Beach at low tide. They will be returned to England for internment and will, therefore, survive the violence and brutality of the end of the war in Europe.

ABOVE LEFT: The generals and the admirals departing Exit E-1 at the Ruquet Valley on June 12 on the DUKW that brought them ashore earlier in the day. The Widerstandsnest 65 bunker is behind them to the left. *National Archives and Records Administration/U.S. Army Signal Corps 111-SC-190157* **ABOVE RIGHT:** German prisoners carry a wounded man on a stretcher toward the water's edge at Exit E-1 on Omaha Beach while a GMC CCKW 2.5-ton Truck drives past. These prisoners are moving out to a landing ship that will carry them to England for internment for the duration of the war. A DUKW sits on the sand at the upper right with men from the 1st Infantry Division gathered in a group behind it. *U.S. Navy photograph, now in the collections of the U.S. National Archives 80-G-252570*

ABOVE LEFT: Medics from the 2nd Naval Beach Battalion and the 261st Medical Battalion, 1st Engineer Special Brigade assist a paratrooper who has been wounded in the right arm as he steps onto the ramp of an LCVP that has pulled up to Utah Beach at high tide. The most seriously wounded troops were evacuated off the beach by landing craft so they could be returned to a hospital in England for critical treatment. Note that the wounded paratrooper is carrying a carton of Chesterfield cigarettes. *U.S. Navy photograph, now in the collections of the U.S. National Archives 80-G-252629* **ABOVE RIGHT:** The paratrooper from the previous photograph is seen here leaning against the portside gunwale of the same LCVP as it motors out to the fleet with five other wounded soldiers on stretchers lying on the deck. It is possible to tell that three of the men on the stretchers are paratroopers because M1942 Jump Jackets and a pair of jump boots are clearly visible. The stretcher patient with his feet closest to the boat's ramp has a German helmet lying on his chest—an obvious souvenir from his experience fighting in Normandy. The LCVP's two deckhands stand by the ramp. *U.S. Navy photograph, now in the collections of the U.S. National Archives 80-G-252446*

ABOVE LEFT: Taken just off of Utah Beach on June 8, this photograph shows an LCVP carrying a group of glider pilots out to the fleet so they can be returned to England. The most noticeable items identifying these men as glider aircrew are the USAAF wings on the left collars of two of the men's shirts. Several noteworthy pieces of equipment can be seen in this photograph including M1 Helmets camouflaged with canvas scrim, M1936 Cartridge Belts, M1936 Suspenders, M1928 Haversacks, and at least one M1936 Musette Bag. Of particular interest are the two souvenir weapons leaning against the LCVP's starboard gunwale just behind the pulley mechanism for the bow ramp: one is a German Kar98k Mauser carbine, and the other is a Soviet SVT-40 Tokarev semiautomatic rifle. **ABOVE RIGHT:** This photograph, taken on June 16, 1944, looks down the length of one of the "whale" causeways of Mulberry A, the temporary harbor built in the American sector at Omaha Beach. An M8 Greyhound Light Armored Car has just executed a left turn onto the causeway, and ahead of it are three M3 Half-tracks towing M5 3-inch Antitank Guns. A sign on the right side of the causeway reads: "Load Limit 25 Ton." To the right, a GMC AFKWX-353 2.5-ton Cargo Truck waits to merge into the flow of traffic going ashore. *National Archives and Records Administration/U.S. Army Signal Corps 111-SC-195879*

ABOVE LEFT: An M3 Half-track from the 612th Tank Destroyer Battalion (Towed) moves down one of the whale floating piers of Mulberry A just off of Omaha Beach on June 16, 1944. In the background, the jack-up legs of two Löbnitz pierheads can be seen as well as the open bow doors of an unloading LST. To the right, five U.S. Army small tugs are moored alongside one another. *National Archives and Records Administration/U.S. Army Signal Corps 111-SC-195881* **ABOVE RIGHT:** Vehicles of A Company, 612th Tank Destroyer Battalion (Towed), 2nd Infantry Division come ashore on Omaha Beach at 5:15 p.m. on June 16, 1944, using one of the whale floating piers of Mulberry A at Saint-Laurent-sur-Mer. The lead M3 Half-track is towing an M5 3-inch Antitank Gun across a section of SMT as it drives onto the beach. *National Archives and Records Administration/U.S. Army Signal Corps 111-SC-195880*

The storm that struck the Baie de la Seine starting on June 19 wreaked havoc on Mulberry Harbor A at Omaha Beach. Here, a Higgins LCS has been pushed up onto one of the whale floating piers, which has been buckled and bent by the pounding surf. Three damaged Löbnitz pierheads can be seen in the background. *National Archives and Records Administration/U.S. Army Signal Corps*

ABOVE: Landing craft pushed up on the shingle of the Dog Red sector of Omaha Beach by the storm on June 21, 1944. LCI(L)-92, which was lost on D-Day, is on the left, with LCT-199 alongside. Beyond them is LST-543. The British LCT-2337 is on the right. *National Archives and Records Administration/U.S. Army Signal Corps 111-SC-193919* **RIGHT:** Three LCVPs from the *Elizabeth C. Stanton*–class transport USS *Anne Arundel* (AP-76) washed up on Omaha Beach during the storm on June 20, 1944. Debris and bodies are strewn on the shingle, and an LCT founders in the background on the left.

ABOVE LEFT: African-American soldiers from the 320th Barrage Balloon Battalion hunt a German sniper at a farmhouse in Saint-Laurent-sur-Mer on June 10, 1944. They are being led by a white officer from Breaux Bridge, Louisiana, named Capt. Samuel S. Broussard, seen here with the vertical white stripe on the back of his M1 helmet and the M1911A1 .45-caliber pistol in his right hand. The man at the far left is armed with an M1 Carbine, while the man just to the right of Captain Broussard is armed with an M1903A3 rifle. *National Archives and Records Administration/U.S. Army Signal Corps 111-SC-190120* **ABOVE RIGHT:** The same group of African-American soldiers is seen here joined by five white soldiers during the hunt for a German sniper in Saint-Laurent-sur-Mer on June 10. Captain Broussard, with M1911A1 Pistol in hand, is coming down a ladder after searching the barn's hayloft. Next to the barn is parked a camouflaged German Army–issue Heeresfahrzeug 6/Feldwagen 43 horse-drawn cart. *National Archives and Records Administration/U.S. Army Signal Corps 111-SC-332023*

ABOVE LEFT: Three U.S. Army paratroopers lay dead in a roadside ditch just outside Sainte-Marie-du-Mont on June 7. The man closest to the camera wears the stenciled stripes of a corporal, and it appears that someone has rifled through his pockets, since the contents are scattered on the ground near him. A box of army K rations sits next to his head. Behind the two gas cans, the body of a third soldier has been covered by a GI raincoat, and the fingers of his left hand are visible. *National Archives and Records Administration/U.S. Army Signal Corps 111-SC-190292*
ABOVE RIGHT: A light-machine-gun section of a weapons platoon from the 1st Battalion, 22nd Infantry Regiment, 4th Infantry Division moves down a sunken lane near Marmion Farm just south of Ravenoville on June 6. The first soldier carries the thirty-three-pound M1919A4 Machine Gun with traverse and elevation mechanism attached to it, and the assistant gunner behind him carries the weapon's M2 Tripod, along with a belt of .30-caliber ammunition. They are passing a German Army–issue Heeresfahrzeug 6/Feldwagen 43 horse-drawn cart as well as two 101st Airborne Division paratroopers. This image is actually a still taken from motion-picture film footage shot by T-4 Weiner of the 165th Signal Photographic Company, the Signal Corps photographer who jumped with the 508th Parachute Infantry Regiment on D-Day. *National Archives and Records Administration/U.S. Army Signal Corps 111-SC-189928*

This photograph shows an Ordnance Maintenance and Repair Company at work in a hedgerow-enclosed Norman field on July 18, 1944. One of the U.S. Army's most important types of supporting units, these companies kept the guns running through the intense demands of combat. Among the more striking features of this image are the 116 M1919A4 Machine Guns lined up for servicing and the virtual mountains of M1903 Rifles piled up in front of the camouflage net in the background. Crates of spare M1919A4 barrels and traverse/elevation mechanisms sit close at hand, and, to the right, piles of M2 and M1917A1 Tripods await servicing. The two seated soldiers on the left are cleaning M1 Garand rifles, and the man to the right with his leg up on a crate is doing the same. *National Archives and Records Administration/U.S. Army Signal Corps 111-SC-191744*

These two soldiers have taken up a position in a typical Norman hedgerow and are armed with two of the army's oldest and newest infantry weapons: the M1917A1 .30-caliber water-cooled Heavy Machine Gun and the M3 .45-caliber Submachine Gun, also known as the "Grease Gun" by the troops. The M1917A1 machine gun had been in the service of the U.S. military for over a quarter of a century by the time it fought in Normandy during the summer of 1944. The Grease Gun, on the other hand, was used in combat for the very first time on D-Day. *National Archives and Records Administration/U.S. Army Signal Corps 111-SC-191283*

ABOVE: These German Army soldiers from Kampfgruppe Heinz of Grenadier Regiment 984, 275 Infanterie Division were killed in action by U.S. soldiers of the 117th Infantry Regiment, 30th Infantry Division near Saint-Fromond just north of Saint-Lô on July 8, 1944. The presence of a spare barrel carrier and a belt of 7.92x57mm cartridges indicates these men were clearly a machine gun team. GIs have obviously searched the bodies thoroughly because their bread bags and gas mask canisters are open, and cigarettes are strewn on the ground around them. Also, their weapons have been removed. *National Archives and Records Administration/U.S. Army Signal Corps 111-SC-191087*

LEFT: Just 8.5 miles southwest of Bayeux and 1,500 feet east of the town of Littry, a Panzerkampfwagen 35R(f) from 3 Kompanie, Schnelle Abteilung 517 sits knocked out in front of a roadside *oratoire* (religious edifice) at the intersection of La Boissellerie and Avenue de la Chasse (present-day D189) on June 20, 1944. This type of vehicle combined the chassis of a captured French Renault R-35 light tank with a Czech-made 4.7cm antitank gun to create a hard-hitting, self-propelled tank destroyer. Schnelle Abteilung 517 was assigned to Grenadier Regiment 916 at noon on D-Day and quickly deployed to the area between Trévières and Bayeux, where it soon came into contact with fighting forces of the U.S. Army's V Corps. The soldier crouching down in front of the Panzerkampfwagen 35R(f) has an M1903 bolt-action rifle slung on his back. *National Archives and Records Administration/ U.S. Army Signal Corps*

LEFT: Second Lieutenant Margaret B. Stanfill is seen here on June 14, 1944, preparing dressings in a tent at the 128th Army Evacuation Hospital at Boutteville, three miles southeast of Sainte-Mère-Église. A veteran of the landings in Algeria in 1942, she was the first nurse to wade ashore when the 128th landed on Utah Beach on the afternoon of June 10 after crossing the English Channel on the Liberty ship *William N. Pendleton*. *National Archives and Records Administration/U.S. Army Signal Corps 111-SC-190305* **BELOW:** A view of the hospital ward of the 42nd Field Hospital near Utah Beach in early June 1944 shows litter bearers, medical orderlies, and casualties. The second man with the helmet marking is clearly a medic from the 261st Medical Battalion, 1st Engineer Special Brigade, which landed at Utah Beach. Note some German Army prisoners/patients in the foreground. *National Archives and Records Administration/U.S. Army Signal Corps 111-SC-190464*

FAR LEFT: A captain from the 307th Airborne Medical Company, 82nd Airborne Division offers a wounded German prisoner a cigarette at the company's medical aid station at La Ferme de la Couture exactly one mile west of Sainte-Mère-Église. Note that he is wearing a Geneva Convention medical brassard on his left arm below his 82nd Airborne Division shoulder patch, as well as a medical roundel painted on the side of his M2 Parachutist's Helmet. The paratrooper at the far left is wearing the right-shoulder U.S. flag unique to the 82nd Airborne during Operation Neptune/Overlord, and an M3 Trench/Fighting Knife in an M8 Scabbard is strapped to his right shin. *National Archives and Records Administration/U.S. Army Signal Corps 111-SC-190289* **LEFT:** Two medics from the 90th Infantry Division administer blood plasma to a wounded German Army *gefreiter* (corporal) at a field hospital near Sainte-Mère-Église. The young corporal's *erkennungsmarken* (identification disc) can be seen lying on the placket of his tunic. The medic on the right is wearing a Geneva Convention medical brassard, which covers the rank stripes on the left sleeve of his M1937 Olive-Drab Flannel Shirt, and a U.S. Army Medical Corps caduceus is pinned to the flap of his left breast pocket. *National Archives and Records Administration/U.S. Army Signal Corps 111-SC-190593*

Medics load wounded Americans aboard C-47 number 42-24195 of 313th Air Transport Squadron, 31st Air Transport Group, Ninth Air Force at Advanced Landing Ground A-21 in Saint-Laurent-sur-Mer, just west of the Easy Red sector of Omaha Beach. The first medical transport from A-21 took place on June 9 at 6 p.m. A field hospital comprising members of the 806th Medical Air Evacuation Squadron was established near the airfield, which facilitated air transport of the wounded, including Norman civilians, to England. *National Archives and Records Administration/U.S. Army Signal Corps 111-SC-190235*

This grenadier from 17 SS Panzer Grenadier Division "Götz von Berlichingen" was killed near the town of Quibou six miles southwest of Saint-Lô when the 2nd Armored Division and the 8th Infantry Regiment, 4th Infantry Division pushed through the area in late July 1944. He was an assistant gunner on a machine gun team, which is why a spare barrel carrier and a belt of 7.92x57mm cartridges are with his body. He wears M42 ankle boots and leggings (*schnürschuhe und gamaschen*), the "44-dot" camouflaged tunic and trousers unique to the Waffen-SS, and an M40 steel helmet (*stahlhelm*). *National Archives and Records Administration/ U.S. Army Signal Corps 111-SC-191302*

A U.S. M7A1 105mm Howitzer Motor Carriage of the 14th Armored Field Artillery Battalion, 2nd Armored Division about to cross the train tracks on the Rue Holgate in the city of Carentan in late June 1944. Nicknamed the "Priest" because of the pulpit-like tank commander's cupola on the right side of the vehicle, the M7A1 provided U.S. Army Ground Forces with a versatile and accurate self-propelled howitzer. *National Archives and Records Administration/US Army Signal Corps 111-SC-190413*

LEFT: An M1 155mm howitzer from the 34th Field Artillery Battalion, 9th Infantry Division is towed on the N-13 by an International Harvester M5 (13t) High-Speed Tractor. The M5 was standardized in October 1942 from the T21, a vehicle based on the tracks and suspension of the Stuart light tank. International Harvester started production of the vehicle in 1942. *National Archives and Records Administration/U.S. Army Signal Corps 111-SC-190385*

BELOW: A group of U.S. Army soldiers from the 313th Infantry Regiment, 79th Infantry Division fraternizing with a Norman woman in Cherbourg on June 26, 1944. The soldier at the far right is leaning on his M1903A4 sniper rifle. This photograph was taken by Pvt. Louis Weintraub of the 165th Signal Photographic Company. *National Archives and Records Administration/U.S. Army Signal Corps 111-SC-191153*

Soldiers of the 79th Infantry Division march a column of German prisoners south along Avenue de Paris/Voie de la Liberté (N2013) at the point where it intersects with Rue Louis Lansonneur (D900) on the southern outskirts of Cherbourg on June 28, 1944. Although pockets of German resistance would hold out for a few more days, the organized defense of the city had reached an end. *National Archives and Records Administration/U.S. Army Signal Corps 111-SC-190810*

ABOVE: The village of Rocquancourt (at the left) is all but lost under a deluge of high explosive as the U.S. Eighth Air Force provides support for ground forces in the area south of the city of Caen. A total of 570 B-24 Liberator heavy bombers from the U.S. Eighth Air Force flew during the initial phase of Operation Goodwood from 6:30 to 8:15 a.m. on July 18, 1944. They struck frontline targets including German troop concentrations, transport targets, and command and control locations in the areas of Soliers, Troarn, Frénouville, the Mézidon railroad marshaling yard, Hubert-Folie, and Fontenay-le-Marmion (at the center bottom). *National Archives and Records Administration/U.S. Army Signal Corps*

FAR LEFT: Staff Sergeant Jack Scarborough of Bossier City, Louisiana, examines the body of a dead German corporal among the fighting positions at Fort du Roule in the defenses of Cherbourg on June 26, 1944. An NCO in the 314th Infantry Regiment, 79th Infantry Division, Staff Sergeant Scarborough is wearing the M42 HBT fatigue uniform and is armed with an M1 Carbine. *National Archives and Records Administration/U.S. Army Signal Corps* **LEFT:** A soldier from the 8th Infantry Regiment, 4th Infantry Division enjoys a drink of Norman cider in Sainte-Mère-Église on June 11, 1944. This image is actually a still taken from motion-picture film footage shot by Sergeant Shelton from Detachment G of the 165th Signal Photographic Company. *National Archives and Records Administration/U.S. Army Signal Corps 111-SC-190325*

"B" in France.
July 11, 1944

The troopers of B Company, 507th Parachute Infantry Regiment, 82nd Airborne Division pose for a group photograph near Utah Beach on July 11, 1944, shortly before the regiment would return to England. B Company, 507th suffered eighty-four casualties during its thirty-five days of combat in Normandy, cutting the company's strength in half. *Courtesy of George H. Leidenheimer*

ABOVE LEFT: The bodies of three *fallschirmjäger* (paratroopers) are piled in the back of a truck at the Blosville Provisional/Temporary Cemetery two miles south of Sainte-Mère-Église. They are about to be buried by French civilians assisting the U.S. Army's Graves Registration Service with the corpses of German war dead. The man at the left with the eye wound wears the collar insignia of *flieger* (private) and the man at the upper right wears the collar insignia of *hauptmann* (captain). These men served in Fallschirmjäger Regiment 6 until their deaths in the intense fighting north of Carentan during the first week of the invasion. This regiment lost just three captains during the initial phase of combat in Normandy. The officer seen here, therefore, is probably Hauptmann Emil Preikschat, who was the battalion commander of 1, Fallschirmjäger Regiment 6 when he was reported missing in action on June 8 somewhere near Sainte-Marie-du-Mont. *National Archives and Records Administration/U.S. Army Signal Corps 111-SC-190600* **ABOVE RIGHT:** This photograph shows what was probably the most famous dump for captured weapons in Normandy. In a field one mile south of Isigny-sur-Mer on the north side of D5 between Hameau de la Madeleine and Ferme de la Petite Fontain, the U.S. Army established a collecting point that was ultimately packed full of vehicles and heavy weapons captured on the field of battle from 2 SS, 17 SS, 352 Infanterie Division, and other German units that fought in Normandy. This view shows the section of the dump where antiaircraft guns, antitank guns, artillery, and tires have been deposited. Easily identifiable here are such pieces of ordnance as the 2cm Fliegerabwehrkanone 30, the 2cm leichte Fliegerabwehrkanone 38, the 8.8cm Fliegerabwehrkanone, the 7.5cm Panzerabwehrkanone 40, the 10.5cm leichte FeldHaubitze 18, and the 15cm schwere Feldhaubitze 18. There is even an 8.8cm Raketenwerfer 43 rocket launcher at the far right. *National Archives and Records Administration/U.S. Army Signal Corps* **BELOW LEFT:** Here is another view of the dump near Isigny-sur-Mer, this one showing the section of the field where armored vehicles were parked. Easily recognizable in this view are at least eight Panzerkampfwagen IV Ausführung H medium tanks armed with the 7.5cm Panzerabwehrkanone 40/3 main gun, including the "898" (center right) of the 8 SS Panzer Regiment 2, 2 SS Panzer Division "Das Reich." The "425" (front and center) is a Panzerkampfwagen V "Panther" from Panzer Regiment 6, Panzer Lehr Division and is coated with *zimmerit* to prevent the use of magnetic antitank mines. Just to the left of the "425" is a Sonderkraftfahrzeug 251 Ausführung D half-track with another one parked next to it. Also recognizable here is a 15cm Schweres infantry Geschütz 33/1 Selbstfahrlafette 38(t) Ausf K (Sonderkraftfahrzeug 138/1) self-propelled howitzer and a Panzerjäger 38(t) Ausführung M "Marder III" (Sonderkraftfahrzeug 138) tank destroyer. *National Archives and Records Administration/U.S. Army Signal Corps* **BELOW RIGHT:** Four female members of a Norman family stand by the gate of their farm to greet passing U.S. soldiers on June 7, 1944. This photograph was taken in the tiny hamlet of Le Guay just five hundred feet east of the road leading out to Pointe du Hoc, and the soldiers are marching on what is now known as D514 in the direction of Grandcamp-Maisy. The first two men wear the Winter Combat Jacket (also known as the "Tanker Jacket") and carry the M1903 rifle.

ABOVE LEFT: Two soldiers from the 2nd Armored Division pause to admire a banner decorating the façade of this electrician's business at 45, Route de Balleroy in Le Molay-Littry 8.5 miles south of Omaha Beach. The Norman people abundantly offered expressions of gratitude like this during the summer of 1944. *National Archives and Records Administration/U.S. Army Signal Corps 111-SC-191171* **ABOVE RIGHT:** On the road between Isigny-sur-Mer and Saint-Hilaire-Petiteville near Carentan, Adjutor Lecanu and his wife, Marie, lay a bouquet of flowers on the body of an American soldier who died after hard fighting in the area between June 9 and 13. A local butcher and World War I veteran, Monsieur Lecanu wanted to express his respect for the man who fell in battle for his freedom. The soldier is an infantryman from the 41st Armored Infantry Regiment, 2nd Armored Division. The scene was not posed, although it was recorded by a number of photographers, one of whom was crudely erased (on the right) by the censor, but who is still visible if you look closely. *National Archives and Records Administration/U.S. Army Signal Corps*

The temporary U.S. cemetery at Marigny is seen here shortly after it opened during the summer of 1944. Located one mile south of La Chapelle-en-Juger and six miles west of Saint-Lô, it was the final burial place for 3,070 U.S. soldiers who lost their lives during the battle for Normandy, mostly during the vicious fighting of the Operation Cobra breakout. Just across the road from the burial area seen here, a cemetery for German war dead was established as well. The U.S. cemetery remained until 1948 when it was closed and the graves relocated to the new Brittany American Cemetery forty miles south near the town of Saint-James. The German cemetery at Marigny is still there with over 11,000 burials in it, mostly men from the Panzer Lehr Division. Today, a memorial marks the field at Marigny where the bodies of U.S. soldiers once lay in early graves. *National Archives and Records Administration/U.S. Army Signal Corps 111-SC-276379*

INDEX